COPY 2

D1035563

FUNNY MEN
OF THE MOVIES

FUNNY MEN

OF THE

MOVIES

Edward Edelson

SⁿH C.

Cumberland Trail Library System
Flora, Illinois 62839

0039/73   COPY 2

Doubleday & Company, Inc.
Garden City, New York
1976

Other Books by Edward Edelson

Visions of Tomorrow
The Book of Prophecy
Great Monsters from the Movies
Healers in Uniform

Library of Congress Cataloging in Publication Data
Edelson, Edward, 1932–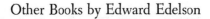
Funny men of the movies.
SUMMARY: Discusses comedy in movies and television
and "funny men" such as Chaplin, Keaton, the Hardys,
Marx brothers, Fields, Jerry Lewis, and Jacques Tati.
1. Comedy films—History and criticism—Juvenile literature.
2. Comedians—United States—Juvenile literature.
[1. Comedy films—History and criticism.   2. Comedians]
I.   Title.
PN1995.9.C55E4   791.43'0909'17
ISBN 0-385-09688-7
ISBN 0-385-09693-3 lib. bdg.
Library of Congress Catalog Card Number 75–14817

Copyright © 1976 by Edward Edelson
All Rights Reserved
Printed in the United States of America
9   8   7   6   5   4   3

Y 791.43
Ede

Contents

CTLS

1

How to Make People Laugh

Being funny is a serious business.

If you don't think so, try to be a comedian yourself. Anyone can get a laugh by doing a pratfall or getting a custard pie in the face. But then what do you do? Slip on another banana peel? Get one more custard pie in the face?

If you tried them, you would find that such simple gags, repeated over and over, would soon fail to bring repeated laughs. Your audience would want something more elaborate—variations in the timing of the pratfalls and the delivery of the custard pies, for example; perhaps a mad chase, full of unexpected incidents. And sooner or later, the audience would want even more: some development of character. Why is the custard pie being thrown? Does the person taking the pratfall deserve the pain? Why is the chase going on, and who deserves to win? Only by meeting those demands would you be able to keep the interest of the audience and keep the people laughing.

And if you did all that, followed that prescription, you would be following the road taken by the earliest funny men of the movies. Film comedy started with very brief sequences that showed the simplest possible situations. One of the first films of all showed nothing more than a man sneezing. For the first viewers, who were fascinated by the very idea of capturing the real movements of people on film, anything was funny, including a scene of a man getting kicked in the seat of the pants, or someone getting a faceful of water.

But that innocent acceptance of everyday scenes soon ended, as viewers became used to the idea of motion pictures. Now they wanted something more. Filmmakers began to shoot longer sequences, with stories to carry the collection of gags. The stories weren't much, and the characters were very basic: a villain with a big, black mustache, a pretty young heroine, a handsome young hero. But at least there was a reason why someone fell down and why someone got a pie in the face—and all of those reasons made the funny parts funnier.

Then audiences began to notice that some faces appeared more than others, and that some actors were funnier than others, and the first movie stars were born. After a while, the audiences began to expect particular actions from some of the stars: one pretty girl would have a special way of smiling, one villain would have a unique way of twisting his mustache. From being nothing more than faces, the actors became personalities—real people, with all the small habits and quirks that make people not only real but funny.

It was more than just actors, of course. The scenes had to be put on film, and the film of the individual scenes had to be put together to make a complete movie. In the early days, when a movie lasted only a few minutes, the actors themselves took care of that. Later, when movies became longer and the plots more complicated, the job was taken over by people who never appeared before the camera; although they could not get a laugh by performing themselves, these people, the directors, could pace a performance and cut the film into scenes that would get the most out of the comedians' antics. Writers were needed too, to invent good plots and (when talking pictures arrived) to provide dialogue.

And that, in a few paragraphs, is the history of film comedy, from its very beginnings to the present day. But what we often tend to forget is that comedy did not start with the movies. When motion pictures came on the scene, comedy was many centuries old. The tradition stretched back through countless generations of clowns and jesters, in circuses, traveling shows, and music halls. But almost all of these funny men who performed before the coming of motion pictures are forgotten today. They made people laugh, but the performance that caused the laughter vanished without a trace as the audience left.

The movies, for the first time, offered a chance to capture the performances forever, so that millions of people could see them even years afterward. And the movies offered another advantage: if the comedian did not get his act quite right the first time, he could do it again, so that the film showed the performance at its best.

But there was a disadvantage. Before films, a comedian could make an excellent living with a limited set of gags. He could travel from town to town, doing the same act over and over again, knowing that the act would be new to most audiences. Movies changed that. Once an act was on film, many different audiences would see it. The next time, they would demand something new.

For a lot of comedians, that was the end of a film career. They simply couldn't provide the endless variety that the film audience demanded. Those who succeeded all did it in the same way: each established a personality that the audience could identify with. Many of those personalities can be summed up in a phrase. Charles Chaplin was the Little Tramp. Buster

9

Keaton was the Great Stone Face. Whatever the personality was, it gave an added dimension to the scenes on the screen, making the comedy even funnier.

But the greatest comedians, such as Chaplin and Keaton, gave the audiences something more. Many comedians can make an audience laugh. A few can make the audience laugh in a way that is different—a way that casts a new light on life. The greatest comedy, like the greatest tragedy, is truly a serious business. We laugh until we cry—and then we realize that the tears are as real as the laughter. The gift to capture that sort of meaning in comedy has been given to very few comedians, and they are ranked at the top of their field.

But perhaps it does not pay to take comedy too seriously. All that most people want from a comedian is some refreshing relief from a world that is usually far too serious. We are lucky today, because we have the opportunity that no other generation has had—the chance to see some great comedians of days gone by. Nearly a century of great comic performances have been captured for us on film. Some of it is jerky, blurred, and of poor quality, but at least the film still exists. We can see what made our fathers laugh, and even what our grandparents laughed at. We can see how the greatest comedians of our century—and some who are not so great—practiced their art. Sometimes we have to use our imagination and put ourselves in a strange world, a simpler world where movies were silent and times were far less complicated. But if we make that effort, we can enjoy the greatest pleasure of all—a good laugh.

And that makes the serious business of comedy a matter of fun.

2

Keystone Days

Movie comedy really started with Mack Sennett and the Keystone films.

That is an exaggeration, but not too much of one. There was comedy in the movies from the very earliest days. As the twentieth century began and the first moviemakers began to master the new technology of motion pictures, it was inevitable that they would try to make viewers laugh. In the very beginning, there were comic films that lasted no longer than thirty seconds or a minute and showed the simplest situations: chairs collapsing, lamps exploding, and the like. It wasn't much, but it was enough.

And even in those early days, the first comic stars began to emerge. One was Max Linder, a French comedian who made dozens of short films in France. Dressed in top hat, white tie, and tails, Linder always got involved in a simple and usually predictable situation: skiing, skating, cooking—and, of course, things always went wrong. In the United States at the same time—those last peaceful years before World War I began in 1914—a plump, droll vaudeville comedian named John Bunny became a film star by making some 150 short comedies, almost all of which have been destroyed by time and neglect. Starting at a salary of only $40 a week (he was making much more in vaudeville, but had the foresight to see the potential of the movies), John Bunny quickly worked himself up to fame and fortune in just a few years. We might remember him better today if he had not died suddenly in 1915, at the height of his success.

But despite those early successes, movie comedy did not really come of age until a young Canadian of Irish descent by the name of Michael Sinnott came on the scene. Michael, whose family moved from Quebec to Connecticut when he was seventeen, took it into his mind to go into show business. Although he was not blessed with too much talent, Mack Sennett (his show-business name) made a career for himself on the burlesque stages and in the Broadway shows of New York. And on his twenty-eighth birthday, in 1908, Mack Sennett went to work for the Biograph Company, one of the first movie studios, for $5.00 a day.

The movie industry was young and informal in those days, and Mack Sennett, like everyone else, did a little bit of everything. He acted; he was a handyman; he wrote scripts; he directed some films. And he looked and listened.

One of the people he listened to was David W. Griffith, a young director at Biograph, who was starting to make movie history. Today, D. W. Griffith is regarded as the first of the great film directors, a man who invented many of the techniques that are still in use today. Griffith had ideas about film drama. Sennett had ideas about film comedy. Griffith may not have learned much from Sennett, but Sennett did learn from Griffith.

By 1912, Mack Sennett was the head of a moviemaking unit at Biograph, grinding out comedies in the quick-time style of those days. Films were short. They were measured in reels. One reel lasted about ten minutes. Many comedies were half-reelers, some were one reel long. A two-reel comedy was something of a major production, but even a two-reeler would be written, shot, and finished in a few days. Mack Sennett made himself a reputation shooting such comedies, and he was soon lured away from Biograph to a new studio, the Keystone Film Company, created just for him.

Sennett was always fond of a good story, and in later years he liked to relate how he had conned a couple of bookmakers to set him up in the movie business to cancel a $240 gambling debt. In real life, the two gamblers were really solid businessmen, well established in movies, who were smart enough to see profits in financing a young man whose talents had been proved. Anyway, Sennett got what he wanted—a free hand to make the kind of comedies, full of slapstick, that would soon become world-famous.

Sennett's first step was to move Keystone from New York to California. He took with him his star comedienne, Mabel Normand; others on hand were Fred Mace, whom Sennett had met in New York, and Ford Sterling, a comedian from Biograph. Very quickly, Keystone was in business.

Another story that Sennett was fond of telling centered around the arrival of the Keystone troupe in Los Angeles. According to Sennett, the troupe arrived in the middle of a Shriners' parade; the cameras were set up at once, the actors started clowning with the marchers, and the result was the first Keystone comedy. It's a fine story—except that no one has a record of such a parade and such a film. Even so, there was the tiniest germ of truth in the yarn, because one of the trademarks of Sennett and Keystone was the knack of taking advantage of anything that was happening in the neighborhood—an auto race, a dance,

Ben Turpin.
In addition to his magnificently crossed eyes, Turpin had comic
skills, including the ability to do a backward somersault, that few
could match.

even the draining of a reservoir. The Sennett clowns would appear, the cameras (hand-cranked) would grind, and the result would be a comedy. Speed was the keynote; Sennett would boast that some half-reelers had been made in a single day.

To keep up that pace, Keystone needed expert professionals. Sennett had them. Just about every great comedian of those days worked for Keystone at one time or another. There was Mabel Normand, who managed to be both beautiful and funny; Ford Sterling, whose "Dutch" makeup—heavy eyebrows and a funny beard—became his trademark; Ben Turpin, whose magnificently crossed eyes started audiences laughing; Chester Conklin of the drooping mustaches; Roscoe (Fatty) Arbuckle, a big man with a great sense of timing; lanky Slim Summerville; dapper Charlie Chase; hulking Mack Swain—the list could go on and on.

Talent like that might seem a guarantee of success, but Sennett was the man who held it all together, as events showed. Among Sennett's many talents, keeping comedians happy was not the foremost. At one time or another, just about every comedian in the Keystone stable left, thinking that there was more money to be made away from Sennett. None of them succeeded outside of Keystone. (There was one exception—a short, slender Britisher whom Sennett had hired away from a traveling music hall troupe. His name was Charles Chaplin.)

What did Sennett provide? Some magnificent comic inventions, for one thing. It was at Keystone, for example, that the first pie in the history of the movies was thrown into a comedian's face. There are learned debates about who thought up the idea of the pie in the face. Sennett gave the credit to Mabel Normand, and it is true that the first pie on film was thrown by Mabel in *A Noise From the Deep*, released in July 1913, with Roscoe Arbuckle on the receiving end. From then on, it was pies all the way, and every which way.

At first, ordinary custard pies were used. But they didn't

hold up too well, especially for such unique stunts as a pie that did a figure eight before hitting home. So they were prepared specially for the movies, with a thick consistency for throwing. As in every field, there were experts in the art; Fatty Arbuckle could hit a target from ten feet with either hand. But anyone could throw a pie and, in the Keystone comedies, everyone did, establishing a comedy tradition that still exists.

Then there were the Keystone Kops, whose name and mad antics still live on in everyday language. The basic idea was simple: the Kops never did anything right. It was Sennett's timing and the skills of the actors that made the idea work so well. The chief of the Kops was Ford Sterling, done up in his "Dutch" makeup, and the composition of the force was always changing. (For a while, it was Sennett's practice to give every new recruit a trial run as a Kop, just to see whether the new comic was up to the hectic Keystone pace.) There were chases, races, collisions, accidents, tumbles, spills—all done without doubles, of course. If the actors couldn't take the punishment, they just weren't Keystone material. For sheer madness and comic invention, nothing has ever equaled the Keystone Kops.

And Sennett also had a string of camera tricks for his comedies. One of his favorites was the scene where a speeding locomotive stops just short of a car, or of the heroine who is tied to the tracks; Sennett would start with the locomotive at what would appear on screen as the "end" of the scene, then have it back up while the camera ground away. By running the film backward, he got the effect he wanted. To make some scenes, Sennett had the camera cranked extra slowly, so that when the film was run at ordinary speed, the cars and people appeared to careen along at incredible velocities (the appearance of speed was increased even further by editing out every third or fourth frame). Sometimes a road would be made slick with artificial soap, and skilled drivers would skid their cars at a breakneck pace. Considering that everything was being done for real, it was a wonder that injuries were relatively rare.

But all of these tricks, however inspired they were, could not explain the success of the Keystone comedies. After all, anyone could copy a Sennett trick as soon as it was put on film —and he had many competitors and imitators. What Sennett had over all these others was a unique sense of madness and of timing. A Keystone comedy was like nothing else on film. The pace was faster, the gags were more inspired, the actors were more frantic. Above all, Sennett had a great sense of timing, one of the most important talents he picked up in his vaudeville career. He knew that to make audiences laugh, the comedies had to build to a climax, with the gags properly spaced and the tempo climbing to a pitch.

A Keystone comedy chase might seem like utterly unplanned chaos, but in reality it was carefully planned in advance in every detail. A careful pace was maintained as gag followed gag, thrill followed thrill. There was never much time for building up the character of the actors, but the sheer speed and verve of the scenes carried the audience along, gasping, to the grand finale.

For a few short years, Keystone prospered. Sennett introduced another sure-fire idea, bathing beauties, who appeared in bathing suits that were daring for the time (Gloria Swanson got her acting start as a Sennett Bathing Beauty), and the audiences loved it. The studio grew bigger, as more units were added and more comedies were ground out. When Sennett sold the Keystone Film Company in 1917, after some complicated business dealings that gave him a good profit, it seemed that he was just at the beginning of his career. In reality, he had passed the high point of his comedy creations.

What happened? Mostly, films began to grow up. As film audiences grew and movies became longer and more elaborate, movie-goers began to demand more than just wild action. They

The Keystone Kops.
This picture was made long after the early Sennett days, when the Kops were briefly reunited. Ford Sterling, in his "Dutch" makeup, is the chief.

The Sennett Bathing Beauties.
The bathing suits were regarded as daring in those days, and the girls were the prettiest in sight.

wanted film characters they could believe in and sympathize with. And, unfortunately, that was Sennett's weak point. If you wanted action, he could give that to you in abundance. But in a Sennett film, the action was never explained—it just happened. The helter-skelter, mad quality of the early Sennett films gave way to a more controlled, less spontaneous style that was more like other filmmakers but not quite true to Sennett's genius. The great days of Sennett film slapstick were over.

Mack Sennett went on making films for years, into the sound era, before he retired in 1935. He made a fortune, most of which was lost in the great stock market crash of 1929. But his real achievement is recorded on the often faded and flickering reels that preserve the mad chases, insane characters, and wild pie-throwing of the early Keystone days. Mack Sennett has had many imitators since those days, but no one has ever caught the precise tone of his peculiar genius.

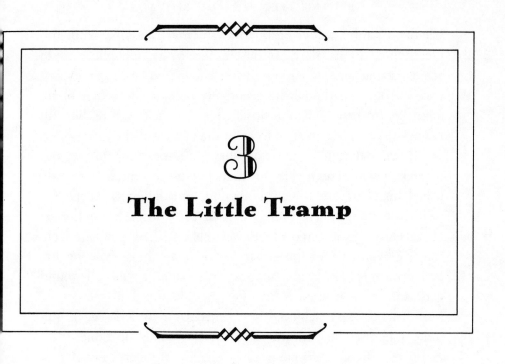

3

The Little Tramp

In 1913, one of Mack Sennett's top comedians, Ford Sterling, left Keystone in dissatisfaction over the money he was getting. Looking around for a replacement, Sennett hired a young British comic who was touring the country with an acting troupe. The salary was $150 a week, which wasn't all that much, and Sennett was glad that it wasn't higher when the comic arrived on the lot.

Bluntly, the new man was a disappointment. To start with, he didn't know anything about making movies; all his experience had been in English music halls, the British version of vaudeville. Then again, Sennett liked comedians who threw themselves into action, got a gag moving quickly and then went on just as quickly to the next gag. The new comedian liked a slower pace, building to a more leisurely climax. Mentally, Sennett wrote off his investment in Charlie Chaplin.

No one ever made a bigger miscalculation. Within months,

21

Cumberland Trail Library System
Flora, Illinois 62839

Charles Chaplin would be hired away from Keystone at an unprecedented high salary. In just a few years, Chaplin was to achieve fame and adoration such as few humans have experienced. And even though he eventually became the center of intense controversy, Chaplin reached a pinnacle where he still reigns—the greatest creative force in the history of the movies.

Even today, it is hard to believe. Charles Chaplin set out to make people laugh. He did that, but he did more: he established his character, the Little Tramp, as a figure of tragedy as well as of comedy. He proved himself to be a master of the art of directing movies, and of writing them. When the sound era came, Chaplin wrote the music for his own films. No one has ever won greater fame and greater acclaim as an all-around genius in his own lifetime than Charles Chaplin did.

No one ever achieved such success from a lower beginning. Charles Chaplin was born in the slums of London on April 16, 1889, the son of music hall performers. His father died when he was young, and his mother could never really support the family. Charles and his brother, Sydney (who later became a comedian in the movies), drifted through the streets of London, hungry and ill-clad; they even spent some time in an orphanage when the money ran out completely.

What saved them from the miseries of the slums was their acting ability. Before his teens, Charles Chaplin was winning laughs on the stages of British music halls. Before long, he was one of the leading comedians in the Fred Karno Pantomime Troupe, perhaps the leading traveling comedy company of its time. The most popular Karno act (some say the greatest vaudeville act ever) was called *Mumming Birds;* it consisted of a series of music hall acts, purposefully bad, who were heckled by members of the audience—the hecklers were actors, of course.

Chaplin played the chief heckler, a tipsy show-goer who fell out of his seat, joined the acts on stage, and finally defeated the Strong Man by tickling him into helplessness. Chaplin was a great hit, as was the entire troupe, and it was inevitable that their successful tours of England would be followed by an American tour. The Karno company set sail, arriving in the United States in September 1910.

Later, members of the troupe would recall that as their ship neared the United States, Chaplin leaped to his feet and declared, "America, I am going to conquer you!" For anyone else, it would have been a bit of idle bravado; for Chaplin, it turned out to be the literal truth.

American talent scouts soon found out that the touring Karno comedians were underpaid by American standards, and member after member of the troupe began to be lured away by offers of more money. Chaplin's turn, as has been mentioned, came in 1913, when Mack Sennett waved the right amount of cash in front of the young comic.

It was only briefly that Chaplin seemed to be a failure. Very quickly, he began picking up the techniques of film comedy in the same way that everyone at Keystone picked them up —in front of the camera. And for his second film, *Kid Auto Races at Venice* (typically for Sennett, the film took advantage of an actual event), Chaplin concocted a costume from bits and pieces around the studio: a baggy pair of Fatty Arbuckle's pants, an ill-fitting pair of shoes (worn on the wrong feet), a jacket that was too small, a derby that perched perilously on his head, a flexible cane, and a tiny brush of a mustache. Soon, Chaplin was to wear that costume in every film. The Little Tramp was born.

In a little more than a year, Chaplin acted in nearly three dozen Keystone comedies. He quickly began to capture audiences. Perhaps his biggest boost came when Sennett decided to make a feature-length film, six reels long instead of the one- or two-reeler that usually came from Keystone. For the film, *Tillie's Punctured Romance*, Sennett brought in a Broadway star, Marie Dressler, to play in the film version of the show in which she had starred on stage. Chaplin was also in the film, playing a city slicker who tried to swindle the country girl, Tillie. Chaplin stole the film from Marie Dressler and was besieged by offers from other filmmakers.

Sennett tried to keep Chaplin, but didn't offer nearly enough money. The winning offer came from a rival studio, Essanay, which offered the astounding sum of $1,250 a week as well as complete freedom to make any film Chaplin wanted to.

Chaplin made fourteen films for Essanay in about one year. He then went to the Mutual Film Corporation (for $670,-000) where he made twelve films. Then came a million-dollar contract (plus a share of the profits) at the First National Film Company, where he made eight films. And finally, Chaplin made eight feature films for United Artists, of which he was a founder, the last of them in 1952.

That is the bare outline of his career. It must also be mentioned that Charles Chaplin at one time was perhaps the most famous person in the world; that he aroused fierce dislike among some people as well as worship by many; that he was almost literally driven from the United States in a wave of controversy; and that the controversy is submerged today in appreciation of his genius. He was even knighted by Queen Elizabeth II of England.

And now it is necessary to explain how all of this could happen to a mere comedian. And the answer is simple: Chaplin was not only a comedian, but something much more.

As a comedian, he was great. One of the best tributes to Chaplin came from W. C. Fields, who was quite a funny man himself and who sat in stony silence as an audience roared at one of Chaplin's films. Asked what he thought of the film, Fields muttered, "He's a ballet dancer, the best ballet dancer that ever lived, and if I get a good chance I'll kill him with my bare hands."

These days, it is difficult for many people to appreciate

Chaplin's comedy. Most of us probably have seen more imitations of Charles Chaplin than the real thing. Many of the Chaplin films we see are now a half-century old; often they are jerky and dim, not much improved by being chopped into small segments. These brief, flickering snippets of film hardly give us an idea of what made Chaplin stand out over all the other great comedians of his time.

Fields was right about one thing: Chaplin was a great ballet dancer. He did miracles with his body, and with props. In Chaplin's hands, everything comes to life: his cane, a ladder, a lump of dough, a clock, a swinging door, a bed. (One of Chaplin's shorts, *One A.M.*, consists almost entirely of his struggle to go to bed while drunk, and ends with a long, hilarious bout with a Murphy bed.) Chaplin could make comic poetry out of the effort to go up a flight of stairs or down a cliff—especially, as was often the case, when someone was chasing him.

Then there was his use of props. In a Chaplin film, nothing was quite what it seemed to be. Perhaps the most famous example of that comes in *The Gold Rush*, where Chaplin, starving in a hut in snowbound Alaska, elaborately cooks and eats a pair of shoes: the nails are removed delicately like bones from a fish, the laces are eaten with gusto like spaghetti. In *The Bank*, Chaplin opens the huge safe with authority—and takes out a mop and pail to wash the floor. In *The Pawnshop*, Chaplin makes such a thorough examination of a clock that a client has brought in—using, among other instruments, a stethoscope and a can opener—that the clock is reduced to junk.

There was no one better than Chaplin at a gag. But if Chaplin had been nothing but a gagman, he never would have become so great. Chaplin could make people laugh, but he could also make them cry. And he could whirl his audience from laughter to tears and back again in moments as no one else has ever been able to do.

Early Chaplin.
Charlie evaluates a clock in *The Pawnshop*, one of his first master-pieces. (*Mutual, 1917*)

At the heart of Chaplin's success is the character of the Little Tramp. From being just another funny figure in a funny costume—every comedian at the time had his own funny makeup —the Little Tramp became a character that audiences could identify with. The Little Tramp was the average man—always on the run to make ends meet, always being looked at with suspicion by authority (cops and bosses never really trusted the Tramp, for good reason), never on the side of the rich and the mighty.

But the tramp was also a figure of pathos—fighting a dog for a bone in *A Dog's Life,* for example—never quite respectable; always yearning for the love of the beautiful girl (played by Edna Purviance in most of the early films) but usually being beaten out by a man who was richer and better-looking.

And the tramp was even more than that—a figure who was so free that nothing was sacred for him. Who but Chaplin could have made a film (*Shoulder Arms*) that asked people to laugh at war in 1918, when millions of men were fighting to the death in the trenches of World War I? Who but the little tramp could make a laughingstock out of everything that ordinary people were supposed to respect—money, the police, all the institutions of society? Who but Chaplin could have audiences rooting for a tramp to bring up a little child (*The Kid*) rather than a rich mother who could provide all the luxuries? In the best sense of the word, the Little Tramp was subversive —by making people laugh and cry, he made them question all the sensible everyday rules that didn't seem so sensible on closer examination.

Critics still write long and learned comments on each of Chaplin's films; it is ironic that the Little Tramp, who was once so subversive, has now become so respectable. But Chaplin was smart enough always to have the last laugh. The Little Tramp never quite took himself totally seriously—there was always a good dose of common sense, as when, in a dream sequence during *The Kid,* the Tramp finds himself wearing wings as an angel and discovers that the wings itch. The Tramp always had enough down-to-earth feelings to know where he itched, and enough sense to scratch.

This common sense was a characteristic of Chaplin in real life. Unlike many other comedians of the silent screen, who quickly lost the fortunes they made, Chaplin held on to his money by shrewd investing. And unlike silent-screen comedians, who were ruined by the coming of sound in the movies, Chaplin made the transition easily—but in a way that only Chaplin could have done.

The sound era arrived shortly after Chaplin had made *The Gold Rush,* a film that many regard as his greatest, and one that has been called the greatest film comedy ever made. Chaplin was working on a movie called *City Lights* when the film world went mad for sound movies. Instead of stopping production and remaking the film with a sound track, Chaplin did it his way: he used sound, but most of the time the only sound was music. Only a few times during the film is sound used as part of the plot—notably, in a scene where the Tramp has swallowed a toy whistle and can't keep from hiccuping during a musical performance, and when some distinguished citizens deliver speeches that are just meaningless squawks.

City Lights had some of Chaplin's finest comic inventions (such as a millionaire who loves the Tramp, but only when he is drunk) and deepest pathos (such as the blind flower girl befriended by the Tramp). It was a triumph.

So was Chaplin's next movie, *Modern Times,* which still used sound sparingly. Despite its age, *Modern Times* is a very up-to-date satire of what we would call automation today. The tone is set by the opening scene, which first shows a flock of sheep and then shows a crowd of men hurrying to work. That tone is maintained as the movie shows the Tramp inevitably losing encounters with modern machinery. Set to work on an as-

Late Chaplin.
Charlie as Adenoid Hynkel, the non-hero in *The Great Dictator*.
(*United Artists, 1940*)

sembly line where his only job is to tighten two nuts, the Tramp eventually goes wild and rushes about tightening everything that looks like two nuts. An automatic feeding machine, designed to keep the workers on the line even during meals, naturally goes crazy when the Tramp tries it. In the finest comment of all, the Tramp actually gets sucked into the assembly line and is run through the gears and works.

It wasn't until *The Great Dictator,* released in 1940, that Chaplin used a conventional sound track. In this film, he played two roles: a little Jewish barber and the megalomaniac dictator, Adenoid Hynkel. Chaplin brilliantly used his resemblance to Adolf Hitler in the film, which was a devastating attack on the brutalities of the Nazis. But the final scene, in which Chaplin literally delivered a plea for world peace to the movie audience, was often criticized by those who felt that it was totally out of place.

The next film, *Monsieur Verdoux,* was even more controversial. In this film Chaplin abandoned the Little Tramp. Instead, he played a dapper, neat gentleman who could be faulted on only one ground: his living was made by killing rich women for their money. The scenes in which Verdoux tries to dispose of his latest wife, played by Martha Raye, were hilarious, but many critics felt that the movie was too talky and resembled a sermon more than a comedy.

One of the last movies in which Chaplin appeared, *Lime-light,* was a nostalgic look backward at the music halls of Chaplin's youth. He plays Calvero, an aging comedian who can no longer make audiences laugh. Calvero saves a young girl (played by Claire Bloom) from suicide, launches her on a successful career, and glories in her success even as his own career plunges downward. In the final scenes, the girl has arranged a benefit night for Calvero. And just for that one night, the old comedian is funny again, making the audience roar with laughter. He takes one final pratfall into a drum and is carried off-stage ill, to die as the girl dances in the limelight. It is Chaplin's farewell to his glories.

Meanwhile, Chaplin had become controversial outside the movie world. Criticized for remaining a British citizen, he was further attacked during the Cold War years for political views that made some people call him a Communist—a ridiculous charge for a man who was a millionaire. Chaplin left the United States in 1952 to live in Europe, and there were many who said it was good riddance.

But as the years went on, a realization grew of what the United States had lost when Chaplin left. It was not until 1972 that he came back for a visit, but then it was in triumph, to accept the cheers of millions and a special Academy Award.

It is impossible to sum up Chaplin in a few words. Decades after he made his last film, critics still have passionate debates about the subtle meanings of the Chaplin films, early, middle, and late. He was a funny man, and much more than a funny man—Charles Chaplin, the one and only, who must be seen to be appreciated.

Cumberland Trail Library System
Flora, Illinois 62839

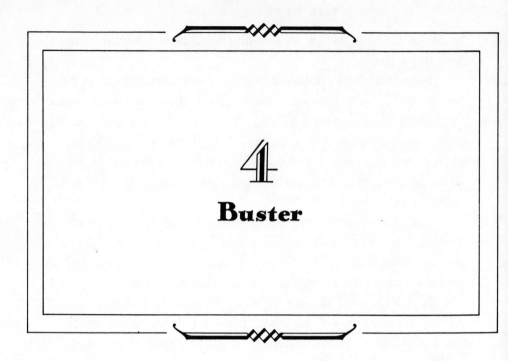

4
Buster

When Buster Keaton was three years old, a cyclone came along one day, sucked him out of a hotel room, carried him through the air for a while, and then set him safely on the ground. That experience could serve as a synopsis of Keaton's life story. Entering films in their early days, Buster Keaton quickly rocketed to the top of the heap. For a decade, he turned out films that were box-office successes and won the critics' praise; for many, he was second only to Chaplin. Then suddenly, almost overnight, his success ended, and Buster Keaton virtually vanished from sight. Only decades later did he make a comeback, both personally and professionally. The storm had set him back on his feet. Today, Keaton's films are famous again, and many critics say he is the rival, even the equal, of Chaplin at his best.

For the first part of his life, Buster knew nothing but happiness. Born into a vaudeville family in 1895, he never went to school for a single day. By the age of one, he made his first appearance by crawling on a stage; when he was three years old, he became a part of the act (whose name was soon changed from "The Two Keatons" to "The Three Keatons"). From the start, Buster had an unusual knack for acrobatic comedy. He got his nickname from the magician, Harry Houdini, who saw young Joseph Francis Keaton fall down a flight of stairs without injury. For a while, the act had his father swinging Buster— billed as "The Human Mop"—around the stage by a suitcase handle attached to Buster's back.

Buster also had an unusual knack for building complicated gadgets, such as a trick fishing line that fooled anglers into thinking they had hooked a big fish. (It was attached to a pier.) He honed his skills by constant vaudeville touring, getting the best kind of training in the things that made people laugh.

The turning point of his life came when The Three Keatons broke up in 1917. Buster was offered $250 a week to continue in vaudeville. Instead, he went to work in the movies for $40 a week.

The man he went to work for was Roscoe (Fatty) Arbuckle, whose acting career was later to be ruined after he was falsely accused of being involved in the death of a young actress. But when Keaton joined him, Arbuckle was at the height of his career, not only starring in comedies but also directing them at his own studio.

As he had learned the skills of vaudeville from his father, Keaton learned the skills of film comedy and directing from Arbuckle. And gradually, the student outdid the teacher. The two-reelers at Arbuckle Studios started as Fatty Arbuckle comedies with Buster Keaton; in the end, they were Buster Keaton comedies with Fatty Arbuckle.

From the start, Keaton played with the same impassive, unmoving expression that people noticed the most about him. It was something he had learned during vaudeville days—if he laughed, the audience didn't, so he went through the wildest scenes without changing expression. But as critics have pointed out, Keaton's face was full of meaning. An emotion that would have been expressed by another comedian with drastic changes of mood was expressed by a slow droop of an eyebrow or a slight twitch of a lip by Keaton. There was plenty of movement in the Great Stone Face for those who watched.

Also visible from the start was Keaton's mastery of gadgets, even the most complex and biggest. In one of his earlier shorts, *The Playhouse,* made in 1921, Keaton showed a theater in which every member of the audience was Buster Keaton, every musician in the band was Buster Keaton, every vaudevillian on the stage was Buster Keaton—even all nine members of a minstrel show were Buster Keaton. The feat was accomplished by using special masks that allowed only one sliver of the film to be exposed at a time. Keaton did each part of the act, then the film was backed up and run through again to get the next part of the act. In an era when the camera was cranked by hand, it took a miracle of timing by Buster and his cameraman, Elgin Lessley, to make it work.

By then, Keaton was both rich and famous, with his own studio. He left Arbuckle, in 1919, to become part of the Metro Pictures Corporation (later MGM), under a contract that gave him $1,000 a week, 25 per cent of the profits his pictures made, and, most important, the freedom to do just about anything he wanted to.

For a while he made short films, two-reelers, at a fast rate: one every two months or so. Even today, these shorts show Keaton's true genius. Every one of them has its unmatchable moments of fine comedy—as in *The Boat,* in which Buster stands proudly on the deck of the boat he has built as it is launched. The boat slides into the water and goes straight under, and Buster goes under with it. In *Cops,* there is one of the maddest film chases of all. The entire city police force, hundreds on hundreds of policemen, is after Buster

Buster Keaton.
A marvelous example of Buster's athletic ability, this pose usually is credited to a full-length feature, *The Navigator,* but was actually from the last of his two-reelers, *The Love Nest.* (*United Artists, 1926*)

(who absent-mindedly used a bomb to light a cigarette and wrecked a parade). The sight of one tiny figure running madly while pursued by an army of bluecoats is unforgettable.

In 1923, Keaton began making full-length features. He was to make two a year for the next six years, and every one of them now is regarded as a classic. Simply to make pictures at this rate was a feat (Chaplin, by comparison, worked for years on each of his feature films). To make comedies of such high quality at such a rate of speed was (and is) unheard of.

In these films, Keaton's mastery of the machinery of the movies—not only props but also the use of the camera—reach new heights. One of the best examples came in *Sherlock, Junior,* released in 1924. Buster, playing a movie projectionist who has lost his girl because of a false accusation, falls asleep while showing a film. His dream double stands up and walks into the film on the screen—only to be kicked off by the villain. Then comes a sequence in which the dream hero moves through a fast-shifting set of movie scenes: when he bends over the edge of a cliff, he suddenly finds himself looking into a lion's mouth; running away, he finds himself in the desert, in the path of a speeding train. Diving into the sea, he lands in a snowbank as the scene suddenly changes. The sequence is still a dazzling technical achievement.

Buster's skill at acrobatics helps create effects that no one else could match. In *Sherlock, Junior,* for example, Buster is in a room, threatened by hoodlums. He jumps out the window through a box containing a dress, somehow manages to put on the dress and a bonnet in his dive, and emerges safely disguised as an old beggarwoman. In *Seven Chances* there is a magnificent scene in which Buster is chased downhill by an avalanche of boulders, some 1,500 of them. Like many of the other daredevil stunts in Keaton movies, this one had to work right the first time, because it would be both expensive and risky to do it over, and it had to be done by Buster alone; hardly ever, even in the most dangerous stunts, did he use a double. Keaton was a magnificent athlete, with immense timing and poise that went perfectly with his physical feats.

Buster's technical mastery of props grew as he made feature-length films. In the two features that are generally regarded as being his best, he used props on the largest scale: in *The Navigator* (1924) the prop is an ocean liner; in *The General* (1926) the prop is a locomotive—indeed, an entire railroad.

In *The Navigator*, the plot has Buster and his girl adrift on the liner; much of the humor comes from the complicated but practical inventions that enable a party of two to live on a ship designed for thousands. The technical achievements in *The Navigator* may be overlooked because Keaton made them seem easy, but one small example will show the effort that went into them: one scene shows a row of cabin doors opening and closing in unison as the ship rolls on the ocean. In real life, of course, the ship was docked and motionless. Keaton used thin wire to connect all the doors so they could be opened and closed at the same time. He used a camera on a weighted tripod that rolled at just the right tempo to give the illusion of the ship rolling. Finally, Buster himself walked at the proper angle while the scene was being shot to make it appear that the ship was rocking to and fro. It took all these elements in unison to create just one of the many special effects in the movie.

In *The General*, a film that represents Keaton at his peak, the plot has Buster as the engineer of a locomotive named "The General," who tries to enlist in the Confederate Army during the Civil War but is refused because his services are more valued on the railroad. His girl and her family, not knowing this, think he is a coward. Buster redeems himself when a band of Union raiders steal The General; he sets off after them and, after a series of adventures, recaptures the locomotive and defeats the enemy.

The General is so rich in invention that it defies descrip-

Buster Keaton.
The cannon has been lighted but won't go off in one of Buster's
best films, *The General*. (*First National, 1926*)

tion. Some scenes must be mentioned: Buster sitting on the drive wheel of the locomotive, suddenly carried up and away as the engine starts—a scene that was potentially very dangerous to shoot. There is Buster peering down the barrel of a cannon to find out why it hasn't gone off; Buster perched on the cow-catcher of the locomotive, carefully flipping a beam of wood ahead to clear away a log that could derail the train (again, a scene that took daring and split-second timing to film). And there is the Union general urging a train to cross a burning bridge, with assurances that the bridge will not collapse—which, of course, it does, in spectacular fashion.

But the gags are only part of the success of *The General*. Keaton captured the Civil War atmosphere perfectly. He used two ancient locomotives and went to Oregon to shoot the film, because only there could he find narrow-gauge track of the kind that existed during the Civil War. The uniforms and the women's dresses were also extremely authentic, so that it seemed as if an old daguerreotype had come to life. No wonder *The General* now is considered to be one of the masterpieces of the silent screen.

The General was followed by other successes, including *Steamboat Bill, Junior*, a film worth mention if only for one of the most amazing gags ever filmed—a scene in which the entire side of a building collapses on Buster, who escapes unharmed because a window fits very neatly around him. To film that scene, which lasted only seconds on the screen, Keaton built a building to measure, with the window placed with utmost precision. (There was only two inches clearance on each side.) His place was marked by nails driven into the ground. The front of the building was made to break away, and then the scene was filmed. It had to be right the first time, and it was.

With pictures such as these to his credit, Buster Keaton's future seemed assured. But his success was to vanish almost overnight. In 1928, he became part of the Metro-Goldwyn-

Mayer studio. And suddenly, he found he had lost the freedom which he had always taken for granted. Instead of doing exactly as he pleased, Keaton had to fight to put his ideas on screen, because studio officials without a tiny fraction of his genius thought that they could tell him the right way to make movies. Their way ruined him.

Keaton's first two pictures for MGM were up to his standard. But as his ideas became diluted with "sure-fire" gags that just didn't work, he fell out of favor. MGM let him go. Personal problems spoiled his attempts at a comeback. He lost his money in the 1929 crash. For a quarter of a century, the great comic genius, perhaps the only comedian who could rank with Chaplin, played bit parts and in cheap film shorts. There was a happy ending of sorts; Keaton eventually worked his way back to star billing, on film and on the stage, and by the time he died in 1966 he had been rediscovered by the film world. But nothing could give him back the lost years.

There are those who say that Keaton was riding for a fall anyway, that he could not have kept up his incredible two-film-a-year schedule, and that his croaking voice would have doomed him when sound films arrived. But as has been noted, Chaplin made the transition from silents to sound movies successfully. Keaton might well have done the same, if he had had the same artistic freedom Chaplin did. We'll never know. But we do know that when Buster Keaton had the chance, he produced film comedies as great as any ever made.

5

Lloyd, Langdon, and Others

In the world of silent comedy, only two comedians were thought to rank alongside Chaplin and Keaton—Harold Lloyd and Harry Langdon. Neither of them quite achieved the artistic success of Chaplin and Keaton, and their films are seldom seen these days, but they did stand out from the host of other funny men who made the 1920s a golden age of comedy. Their ultimate personal fates were quite different—one went up toward prosperity, the other down toward failure, but for a while Lloyd and Langdon rode the crest of success.

Harold Lloyd had to work for his success, and it did not come quickly. He broke into the movies before 1915 in anything but a promising way: Lloyd created a character called Willie Work for Hal Roach, who was Mack Sennett's chief rival, but Roach was so unimpressed that he refused to give Lloyd a raise of only $5.00 a week. Lloyd quit to work for Sennett, but that didn't work out either and he went back to the Hal Roach studio.

41

By then, Lloyd had developed a character called Lonesome Luke who had a vague but suspicious resemblance to Chaplin's Little Tramp. Lonesome Luke may have lacked something in personality, but Lloyd tried to make it up by sheer effort, turning out scores of Lonesome Luke comedies every year. The films, one- and two-reelers, were built on sheer slapstick—pies in the face, breakneck chases, and the like. But there were plenty of other comedians working the same theme, and Lloyd did not really achieve success until he came up with a new character— the bespectacled, slightly absurd but likable young man, who gets into plenty of scrapes, but always manages to get out of them, and who succeeds in the end through a combination of good luck and hard work. It might not sound like an inspired formula, but Harold Lloyd made it work by producing an endless supply of inventive gags and comic situations. If the audience never got terribly involved with the character (as it did with Chaplin), at least Lloyd kept people laughing from start to finish.

That ability to build gags to a peak was best shown in *Safety Last,* a 1923 feature that has one of the most famous gag sequences in film history. For some reason, Lloyd must climb up a building as a "human fly." Higher and higher he goes, despite every comic peril that could be imagined: a net falling on him, entanglement with painters' scaffolding, even a mouse running up his leg. Finally, he grabs hold of the building's clock—only to have the hand move steadily downward toward six o'clock. To top even that, the face of the clock gives way, and Lloyd is suspended by a single spring. And when he reaches the top of the building by a miracle, he is bashed in the head and wanders dizzily along the parapet until he somehow is deposited safely on the roof. For sheer thrills, no scene can top the sequence.

The same is true of the climactic scene in *The Freshman,* a 1925 college comedy that has Lloyd in various inspired se-

Harold Lloyd.
Safety Last, with Harold hanging from the hands of a clock after a perilous climb to the top of a building. (*Pathé, 1923*)

quences: as a human tackling dummy for the varsity football team, as an embarrassed swain at the college dance, where his hastily made tuxedo keeps coming apart on the dance floor, and so on. It all leads up to the Big Game, in which the coach is forced to play Lloyd (who is the water boy) because every other player is injured. Naturally, Lloyd scores the winning touchdown, but only after a series of misadventures: he runs for a touchdown—but with someone's hat, not the football. He does run for a touchdown with the football (but only after he manages to pick it out of a crowd of balloons that a vendor has let go) but throws the ball down just short of the goal line when he hears a factory whistle blow. And finally, he scores a real touchdown by scooping up a fumble and just being over the goal line when a massive pileup of players is untangled.

Lloyd's humor was rather uncomplicated, compared to the complex films of Chaplin and Keaton, and his life was the same. While Chaplin was driven from the United States and Keaton descended to poverty, Lloyd retired gracefully with the fortune he had made. If there was one theme that ran through the Harold Lloyd comedies, it was the classic American success story—the story of the young fellow, full of ambition and ready to work hard, who managed to win his fortune despite all adversities, even though he may not have been too bright. That story may seem rather hollow in these more complex times, but Americans really believed it in the days when Harold Lloyd was making comedies. And Lloyd's own life story was that success saga come true.

It was just the opposite with Harry Langdon, a comedian who was at the very top for a few years, but whose name (and whose films) are now neglected by all but the most dedicated fans of film comedy. After a brief and spectacular success, Langdon plummeted to failure; the reason, most critics said, is that Langdon achieved his success by letting others direct his pictures, and failed when he decided that he could be his own director: the character he created was funny, but Langdon could not create a sustained setting for that humor.

Compared to his rivals, Langdon got a late start in the movies. He did not join Mack Sennett until 1923, after a long career in vaudeville. Sennett soon realized that Langdon, although his humor was not of the breakneck, slapstick type that the Sennett studios featured, still had a special talent, and some of the top directors and writers in the studio were assigned to work with Langdon.

These men—notably the writers Harry Edwards and Arthur Ripley and the director Frank Capra—built their films around the character suggested by Langdon's makeup, a heavily powdered face with wide, staring, innocent eyes. It was a baby face on an adult body, and most of the comic situations in Langdon films get their laughs by showing this helpless, pathetic figure trying to compete in an adult world. Capra called the Langdon character "the helpless elf whose only ally is God," and there were such scenes as Harry trying to fight off a tornado by throwing pebbles at it (*Tramp, Tramp, Tramp*, made in 1926); Harry rubbing his chest with what he thinks is camphor but is actually Limburger cheese as he rides on a bus (*The Strong Man*); Harry trying to kill an inconvenient fiancée but stopping because he sees a sign that says "No Shooting" (*Long Pants*, made in 1927).

All these films were made after Langdon had been hired away from Sennett by First National Pictures, which gave him not only a lot of money—$7,500 a week—but also complete control over his pictures. As long as Langdon didn't use that control, but followed the advice of Capra, Ripley, and Edwards (who followed him to First National), he was a hit. When he began to direct his own films, his success ended abruptly. The critics found that Langdon the director lacked a sense of timing, that although there were excellent gag sequences in movies like *Three's a Crowd* (made in 1928), most of the scenes were al-

Harry Langdon.
A sentimental moment in *Tramp, Tramp, Tramp*. The girl is Joan
Crawford. (*First National, 1926*)

lowed to run on and on, until the humor was worn out. His next movie, *The Chaser,* got the same reaction. Audiences stopped laughing and Langdon was on a quick downhill slide. His personal problems (a marriage had broken up), his tendency to spend too much money on his films, and—not least—the coming of sound films speeded the process. A mere five years after Langdon had rocketed to film success, he was a has-been.

His movie career did not end. All through the 1930s and well into the 1940s, Langdon made a series of low-cost two-reel comedies for a variety of studios. There are flashes of the old Langdon magic in some of these short comedies, but most of them are run-of-the-mill at best. He was still working in films when he had a stroke and died in 1944.

Chaplin, Keaton, Lloyd, and Langdon (most critics list them in that order) were the big four of silent-screen comedy, but there were many other comedians who flourished at the same time. It was an era of apparently insatiable demand for film comedy, and the supply did meet the demand. The funny men (and women) who worked to meet that demand may not have reached the heights of the big four, but there are bits and pieces in their films (and sometimes entire films) that are as funny as anything put on the screen.

Some have already been mentioned, such as the stable of comedians assembled by Mack Sennett: Mabel Normand, whose career was disastrously short; Ford Sterling, Fatty Arbuckle, Al St. John, and many others. There was the group assembled by Hal Roach, who worked hard at being as funny as Mack Sennett but never quite made it. Many of his comedians had previously been with Sennett—Snub Pollard, Charley Chase, Will Rogers (yes, he made movies as well as starring on stage) and more. There were comedians whose names are almost forgotten by all but film buffs today, but who were acclaimed in their time: Larry Semon, Bobby Vernon, and others.

The key event in the lives of all these comedians—indeed,

of everyone in the movie industry—was the coming of sound. Overnight, comedians and everyone else had to learn a new vocabulary. In the silent comedies, .the story was told by facial expression and pantomime. Now the story could be told in words; what comedians *said* suddenly became perhaps more important than what they *did;* the writer gained a new importance; the rules of the whole game were changed.

It was not an easy transition for most comedians. As has been noted, several years went by before Chaplin began using sound in his films, and even then he never lost his basic reliance on the techniques of the silent screen. Many lesser comedians (and some of the greater ones) found that their careers had come to an abrupt halt with the sound era. It is certainly more than a coincidence that both Buster Keaton and Harry Langdon fell from the heights at just about the time that the movies began to talk. Some comedians who had never been in films, on the other hand, found just as suddenly that they had a whole new career opened to them. And a completely different kind of film comedy, one that was carried by its dialogue, was born.

Film comedy certainly lost a great deal when sound came in. There are some critics who believe that the silent comedies were the "purest" of all, because they relied entirely on techniques that could be used only in the movies. That might have been true in the early days, when Hollywood was baffled by the new requirements of movies that talked, and when directors often did little more than set up a camera in a fixed location to make a dismal screen version of a stage comedy where all the actors stood on one spot and talked endlessly. (The directors can be partially excused for this on the grounds that good mobile microphones had yet to be developed.) But soon, a new breed of filmmakers who knew how to make use of sound without sacrificing the special opportunities of film came to the front. One great era of film comedy had indeed ended, but another great era had begun.

6

Stan and Ollie

When Charles Chaplin was hired away from the touring Karno troupe by Mack Sennett, his place in the troupe was taken briefly by a young British vaudevillian named Stan Jefferson. But the act did not do well without Chaplin and, after drifting from one act to another, Stan Jefferson (perhaps inevitably) turned to film work. After working with various studios for a few years, Stan Laurel (as he was now calling himself) signed on permanently with the Hal Roach studio in 1926.

One of the comedians who appeared in Stan Laurel two-reelers was a stout young Georgia-born American who had had a similarly checkered career in the movies, sometimes playing villains, sometimes playing comedians. His name was Norvell Hardy, but he called himself Oliver Hardy (his father's name); everyone else called him "Babe."

After a while, some began to notice that Stan Laurel and Oliver Hardy together in a film were funnier than they were working separately. And just like that, in an amazingly accidental fashion, one of the greatest and most durable comedy teams in Hollywood history was born. Laurel and Hardy had arrived.

That is, they had arrived as far as audiences were concerned. It took the critics a much longer time to decide that Laurel and Hardy deserved to rank among the funniest men of the movies. Indeed, it was not until the boys had finished their film career that they won real critical acclaim. True, the critics knew that Laurel and Hardy were invariably box-office hits, and that Stan and Ollie were known and loved all over the globe, but critics tended to discount that success as a case of sheer slapstick winning out over good taste. It was only when the critics had time to sit down and give a careful look that they realized what audiences had known all along—that Stan Laurel and Oliver Hardy had created two of the most remarkable comedy characters in the history of films.

One reason for this critical neglect is the sheer volume of Laurel and Hardy movies. During their career, which lasted into the mid-1940s, Stan and Ollie made over 100 films, from two-reel comedies to full-length features. In 1928 and 1929 alone, the boys turned out the amazing total of twenty-three two-reel shorts for Hal Roach. Inevitably, there were dull spots and unfunny moments in some of those films, and the critics tended to judge Stan and Ollie by their low points. In addition, the team made nothing but full-length features for the second half of their career, and almost everyone agrees that Laurel and Hardy were not at their best in the longer movies.

In a two-reel comedy, Stan and Ollie could take a single comic idea and develop it to the full without strain. But longer films required more than just a single gag idea; more elaborate plots had to be concocted, other actors had to be introduced, and so on. A lot of what was added can be described as just padding.

Some of the padding was quite plush, however—romantic heroes, songs and dances, costume drama and the like. The full-length features have funny moments that are as good as any in the two-reelers, but sometimes a viewer can get impatient waiting for those moments to arrive.

None of this should obscure the boys' real achievements in comedy, which few other funny men could match. Just to mention one point, Stan and Ollie made the transition from silent film to the talkies without skipping a beat. Without losing the ability to develop a gag—or a series of them—in purely visual terms, they were able to add depth to their characters through dialogue.

And what characters they were—two of the most lovable incompetents ever to blunder their way across the screen. Disaster follows Laurel and Hardy as inevitably as the night follows the day. Stan Laurel's incompetence is evident at first glance. He is the kind of innocent who must pause and scratch his head when asked the time of day, and one who is certain to give the wrong answer to that question even when he is in a clock factory. Oliver Hardy is just as bad, but he causes more trouble because he is the sort of wrongheaded person who is sure that he is in the right. Every time Ollie stands watching Stan do something wrong and then says, "Let *me* do it," you can be sure that even worse is to follow. And when the boys work in tandem, a job that would be child's play for most people becomes a sure prescription for catastrophe.

For example, *The Music Box,* one of their best shorts (and their only film to win an Academy Award) is built on the simplest of ideas: Laurel and Hardy have to deliver a piano. Naturally, the house where the delivery must be made is at the top of an apparently endless staircase that runs up a terraced hillside. Hardly any dialogue is needed, and the most important sound effect is the tiny jingle that comes from the piano as it bounces

Laurel and Hardy.
The film is *The Music Box*, which won an Academy Award, and the boys are trying to get the piano up the flight of stairs, with their usual skill. (*Roach-MGM, 1932*)

Laurel and Hardy.

The film is *Double Whoopee,* the girl is Jean Harlow, and she is about to have her skirt removed as Stan slams the door of that taxi. (*Roach-MGM, 1929*)

down the steps—and, of course, it does bounce down the steps time and again after the boys have expended infinite effort to push it up.

First they run into a baby carriage that is coming down the staircase; the piano eludes their efforts to get to one side, and goes jingling to the bottom. Starting again, they get almost to the top of the stairs when a cop calls for them to come down. The piano comes down, too.

Once more they go sweating up the hill, only to be met halfway by a pompous professor who insists that he will not step aside to let the piano pass. The professor loses that argument as well as his hat, which is knocked into the street to be demolished by a passing car. The boys reach the top, but their attention wanders just a bit and the piano goes jangling down the steps again, with Ollie hanging on for dear life.

Finally, they are at the top once more, to be told by a mailman that they could have driven to the house by a side road. So, naturally, they take the piano down the stairs, load it on their truck, and drive it to the house. The rest of the film shows the boys' equally disastrous attempts to get the piano into the house. Ultimately, they succeed, only to find that the professor they insulted is the man who is having the piano delivered.

Another film that builds to disaster is *Helpmates*, a short made in 1931 that has Ollie enlisting Stan's help to clean up his house in preparation for the return of his wife. Stan, always helpful, carefully demolishes everything in sight, including all the dishes in the kitchen, Ollie's wardrobe and, finally, the house itself (by using gasoline to start a blaze in the fireplace). At the end, Ollie is sitting in the ruins of his home, which no longer has a roof, and Stan is getting ready to leave. Ollie has only one last request: "Would you mind closing the door? I'd like to be alone." Stan closes the door as the rain begins to fall on Ollie.

Helpmates has some dialogue that is typical of the boys at their best. At one point, they are talking on the telephone, and Stan explains that he has been bitten by a dog. "Where?" Ollie asks. "Here," Stan says, lowering the telephone to the appropriate spot. At another point, this exchange occurs:

STAN: "You know, if I had any sense I'd leave."

OLLIE: "Well, it's a good thing you haven't!"

STAN: "It certainly is!"

Then Stan scratches his head as he tries to figure out what he has said.

Other disasters include Stan, in *The Bohemian Girl,* a full-length feature of 1936, trying to fill some wine bottles by siphoning wine out of a keg with a hose. Stumped about what to do with the hose as he changes bottles, Stan puts it into his mouth. As time goes by, more and more of the wine is going into Stan, less and less into the bottles, with predictable results. And there is the scene in *Saps at Sea,* made in 1940, in which Stan and Ollie prepare a repulsive meal (twine for spaghetti, liquid tobacco for coffee, talcum powder for biscuits) to give to the criminal who is holding them prisoner—only to have to eat the meal themselves.

If disaster (self-created) is one theme of Laurel and Hardy comedies, another is a slow and calculated progress toward chaos and destruction. For example, in *The Perfect Day* (a two-reeler built entirely on the boys' efforts to leave for a picnic), there comes a moment when Ollie throws a jack at Stan and breaks a neighbor's window. The neighbor strolls over and, quite leisurely, throws a brick through the windshield of the boys' car. Just as deliberately, Stan throws a brick through the window of the neighbor's house. The neighbor does the same to a window of Ollie's house. The sequence breaks off there (the film ends when the boys, after a number of false starts, finally drive away —only to have the car sink into a bottomless puddle), but the progression of slow, studied destruction is carried much further, with hilarious results, in other comedies.

In *Two Tars,* Stan and Ollie are sailors on leave who get caught in a traffic jam and get into an argument with the motorists around them. Before long, everyone is ripping off headlights, tearing off wheels, bending fenders and otherwise ruining autos—all with a slow, careful thoughtfulness that adds immeasurably to the humor. In the end, the cars drive away in one of the most outrageous processions ever filmed, each car showing the effects of the damage. The topper comes when the boys drive into a railroad tunnel and meet a train; they emerge at the other end driving a car that now is wafer thin. And in *You're Darn Tootin',* the boys get into a round of shin-kicking and pants-tearing that involves a dozen passers-by.

But the greatest of these scenes of mutual destruction comes in *Battle of the Century,* in which Laurel and Hardy made what Stan called "a pie picture to end all pie pictures." To film the final scene, the studio bought out one day's entire production of the Los Angeles Pie Company, four thousand pies. Before the film is over, every one of those pies is thrown into someone's face.

The pie-throwing scene, now famous to every Laurel and Hardy fan, begins with an argument over a banana peel—an argument that takes place near a parked pie wagon. For reasons of his own, the driver of the pie truck hits Ollie with a pie. Stan hits the pieman with a pie in retaliation. A stranger, pausing to settle the argument, gets a pie in his face and throws one for revenge. The scene builds steadily, with passers-by and occupants of the shops on the street being involved one by one, and joining in the pie fight. Before long, the air is full of flying pies, which hit people from every angle and with every comic variation imaginable. At the very end, a policeman arrives to arrest the troublemakers. He slips on the banana peel that started the whole thing and vanishes down a manhole.

In all of their movies, Laurel and Hardy were able to play against the stable of excellent comedians collected by Hal

Roach. Billy Gilbert was the stuffy professor in *The Music Box,* and Edgar Kennedy played a gouty father-in-law in *The Perfect Day.* Any number of skilled professionals, including Charlie Hall, Thelma Todd, and Mae Busch, can be seen in Laurel and Hardy films. But the most reliable of all was James Finlayson, a mustachioed, bald-headed Scotsman with a pair of magnificently eloquent eyebrows, suitable for registering dismay and indignation as Stan and Ollie did their stuff. Finlayson shows up in many Laurel and Hardy movies, an ideal foil for the boys.

There is a comic genius behind all this fun—none other than Stan Laurel. Empty-headed though he may have appeared on the screen, Stan in real life was a master of all the serious business that is involved in making audiences laugh. He developed many of the gags; he played a key role in the important but little-noticed art of cutting film so that the gags reel off at the right tempo (you have to give the audience time to laugh at one gag before the next one appears); and, although he never was credited as director of any of the Laurel and Hardy movies, Stan was usually around to help the director shoot the film. Ollie, by contrast, was a happy-go-lucky type who was content to spend most of the time between movies on the golf course or at a swimming pool.

Despite this unequal division of labor, Stan Laurel and Oliver Hardy meshed together perfectly. One of the reasons why their films are such fun is that they were instinctively good comics; one of their directors said that they could improvise a scene as long as there was film in the cameras. They knew each other; they knew how to be funny; they liked being funny—and the results showed on the screen. Although the boys may have feuded constantly in their films, the situation in real life was very different; they appreciated each other, both as comedians and as persons. There are several descriptions of Stan Laurel, watching a Laurel and Hardy comedy at a private showing and breaking up at the antics of Oliver Hardy.

But even the best years must end. The boys kept on making films into the 1940s, but their last films, done away from the Hal Roach studios, are a pale shadow of their really funny efforts. It was the same sort of trouble that Buster Keaton had run into—there were fussy executives who thought that they knew comedy better than the best comedians of the screen. The last Laurel and Hardy movie, made in Italy under the title *Atoll K* in 1950, was an utter disaster that the boys simply tried to forget.

But even when their filmmaking days were over, there were reminders of how well they had done. One such reminder came in 1953, when Laurel and Hardy were on a tour of the British Isles. Their boat docked in Cobh, Ireland, and they looked out to see the pier swarming with hundreds of admirers. And just then, they heard their theme song ringing out on all the church bells of the city. They cried.

Babe Hardy died in 1957. Stan Laurel died in 1965, but not before the film community showed its respect with a special Academy Award for his contributions to film comedy. But the real tribute to Laurel and Hardy comes whenever any of their great comedies are shown. They are very funny men, and they can still make audiences laugh as few comedians have ever been able to make people laugh.

7

The Marx Revolution

"Members of the faculty; faculty members. Students of Huxley and Huxley students. I guess that covers everything. Well, I thought my razor was dull until I heard this speech. And that reminds me of a story that's so dirty I'm ashamed to think of it myself. As I look out over your eager faces, I can readily understand why this college is flat on its back. The last college I presided over, things were different. I was flat on my back. . . ."

It is the opening scene of *Horse Feathers,* and the speaker at a college convocation is, naturally, Quincy Adams Wagstaff, the most outrageous college president on record. But you should not be surprised. Quincy Adams Wagstaff is Groucho Marx, and he is always outrageous. In *Cocoanuts,* Groucho is the most outrageous real estate salesman on record. In *Duck Soup* he is the most outrageous president of a country on record. In *A Day at the Races* he is the most outrageous physician on record.

But if you think Groucho is mad, try Chico, who is just as

outrageous, but in an Italian accent, or Harpo, who is even madder without ever saying a word. Put them all together and you have the Marx Brothers, the maddest, most outrageous, and possibly the funniest comedy team of all times.

But there is method to their madness. The Marx Brothers have a specialty—demolishing any pretensions to dignity. Anyone who enters a Marx Brothers movie riding a high horse will exit on foot, usually having been kicked in the behind, trailing the rags of his (or her) dignity in the dust.

There is Groucho talking to a lovely lady in *Monkey Business:* "I know. You're a woman who's been getting nothing but dirty breaks. Well, we can clean and tighten your brakes, but you'll have to stay in the garage all night."

There is Chico, in *A Night at the Opera,* describing how they flew nonstop over the Atlantic: "The first time we start, we get halfway across when we run out of gasoline and we got to go back. Then I take twice as much gasoline. This time we were just about to land, maybe three feet, when what do you think? We run out of gasoline again. Then back we go and get more gas. This time I take plenty gas. Well, we get halfway over, when what do you think happen? We forget the airplane. So we got to sit down and we talk it over. Then I get the great idea. We no take gasoline. We no take the airplane. We take a steamship. And that, friends, is how we fly across the ocean."

And there is Harpo, who needs no words. When Groucho says, "You can't burn the candle at both ends," Harpo reaches into his coat and pulls out a candle—burning at both ends. When a panhandler says, "Say, buddy, could you help me out? I'd like to get a cup of coffee," Harpo reaches into his coat and pulls out a cup of coffee. And when a cop tries to bully Harpo by showing him a badge, Harpo opens his coat to show a lining covered with badges.

None of it makes sense, but all of it is funny. To see a Marx Brothers movie is to enter a special world where three madmen are running loose, totally out of touch with reality and yet somehow more in charge of what is happening than anyone who seems to be in charge. By breaking all the rules, by insulting everyone in sight, and doing all the things that everyone else secretly wants to do, the Marx Brothers make us realize just how crazy the world really is. It is comedy at its very best.

All of this began, as much of the best film comedy did begin, in vaudeville. To start with, there were five Marx Brothers —Julius. Adolph, Leonard, Milton, and Herbert, who became, respectively, Groucho, Harpo, Chico, Gummo, and Zeppo. The mother of this brood was a marvelous lady named Minnie Marx, who was determined that her sons would succeed in show business. (There was something of a show business tradition in the family; an uncle was Al Shean, who was half of the celebrated vaudeville team, Gallagher and Shean.)

The early years, around the turn of the century, weren't easy. It took years of work and boos and flops to develop the peculiar genius of the Marx Brothers. But by 1924, the brothers were hits on Broadway in a show called *I'll Say She Is!*, which established them firmly as stars.

Their first movie, made in 1929, was *Cocoanuts* (that's how they spelled it then), a film version of a stage show in which the brothers had been. They were the four Marx Brothers then, Gummo having dropped out of the act already. Paramount Pictures had a studio in the section of Queens called Astoria, just across the river from Manhattan, and the company was able to offer Broadway stars an unbeatable deal. They could take the train to Astoria in the morning to shoot a film and be back on stage at night for their Broadway shows. Unfortunately, space was limited at the Astoria studio, and the films made there tended to be unimaginative, static versions of the stage plays. So it is with *Cocoanuts*.

The movie is supposed to take place in Florida, but it is obviously being shot indoors throughout, usually on a set that is

The Marx Brothers.
Their first film, *Cocoanuts*. That is Margaret Dumont standing be-
low Groucho. (*Paramount, 1929*)

painfully unreal. And the actors tend to stand in one place, just as they would on stage. But with all these faults, *Cocoanuts* is still funny as only a Marx Brothers movie can be funny.

For one thing, *Cocoanuts* saw the birth of one of the great teams in movie history—Groucho Marx and Margaret Dumont. Miss Dumont, every inch a lady and the image of dignity, was to appear in film after film as the perfect foil for Groucho, who was every inch a cad and the image of indignity. The dialogue from *Cocoanuts* set a standard that would be followed faithfully in later movies:

Groucho: Your eyes, they shine like the pants of a blue serge suit.

Margaret: What? The very idea. That's an insult.

Groucho: That's not a reflection on you; it's on the pants.

And later in the same love (?) scene, Groucho woos Margaret by saying, "I'll meet you tonight under the moon. Oh, I can see you now, you and the moon. You wear a necktie so I'll know you."

The plot, such as it is, has Groucho as a Florida hotel owner who is also trying to sell real estate. Harpo's role cannot be described; he simply sprints through the film madly, drinking ink and eating glass. Chico plays a friend of Groucho who ruins a land auction by bidding up the price as he has been trained to do, even though no one is bidding against him. Zeppo does little more than walk on and walk off.

The next movie, *Animal Crackers*, was another of the brothers' Broadway hits filmed at the Astoria studio. The film has its faults, but those are outnumbered by its hilarious moments, and it earns its place in history by having Groucho sing, "Hooray for Captain Spaulding," which became his theme song. Unhappily, the movie has a plot that pivots around a famous painting that is stolen, hidden, and stolen again, while the audience yawns and waits for the Marx Brothers to come back on stage.

After *Animal Crackers,* the brothers moved to Hollywood for good. The next three films—*Monkey Business* in 1931, *Horse Feathers* in 1932, and *Duck Soup* in 1933—are regarded by many of their fans as the funniest they ever made and are certainly three of the best comedies ever put on film.

Monkey Business starts with the brothers as stowaways on an ocean liner and takes off from there. One of the scenes that makes the film so memorable has Harpo, on the run from pursuing officers, getting into a Punch and Judy show, where he does an unmatchable imitation of a puppet that has to be seen by anyone interested in the art of clowning. There is another scene in which Harpo enters in mad pursuit of a blonde, spots another pretty girl walking by, and exits in mad pursuit of her. And there is Groucho responding to the question, "Are you a doctor," with the reply: "Of course I'm a doctor. Where's the horse?" And there is Chico, asked, "Would you like to see where he sleeps?" and answering, "Aw, I saw that. That's the bunk." Most of the rest of the film defies explanation.

Horse Feathers has the brothers demolishing the campus of Huxley College (whose traditional rival is Darwin). Groucho is the college president and Zeppo is his son, a student. ("I married your mother because I wanted children," Groucho tells him. "Imagine my disappointment when you arrived.") Harpo and Chico play two nobodies who are mistaken for football players, and who manage to win the big game at the end.

Magic moments include Harpo walking by a card game, hearing someone say, "Cut the cards," and doing just that—with a cleaver; and Chico explaining that last week "I got a coed with two pairs of pants," not to mention Groucho teaching a biology class (on the white phagocytes) with Harpo and Chico among the students. The film never slows down and never stops being funny.

Duck Soup is probably the funniest movie the Marx Brothers made. This time the subject is patriotism and war, and the

Marx Brothers make both seem foolish. It takes place in Free-donia, a country that has gone broke and counts on Mrs. Teasdale (Margaret Dumont) to pay the bills. She will, but only if the country accepts Rufus T. Firefly (Groucho) as president. Louis Calhern, an actor who distinguished himself in many films, provides the menace by playing the ambassador of Sylvania, a country that wants to conquer Freedonia. Harpo and Chico play a pair of the worst spies in history, while Zeppo is Firefly's secretary. (This was Zeppo's last movie; realizing that he could not match the madness of the other three brothers, he quit films.)

It is hard to pick out the best parts of this inspired film, but mention should be made of the zaniest cabinet meeting ever held (Minister of War: How about taking up the tax? Groucho: How about taking up the carpet. Minister: I still insist we must take up the tax. Groucho: He's right. You've got to take up the tacks before you take up the carpet.), and the celebrated scene, imitated countless times since, in which Harpo, dressed like Groucho, stands in front of what he thinks is a mirror. Actually, there is no mirror, just Chico, also dressed exactly like Groucho, who follows his movements with hilarious precision. Groucho himself finally shows up to bring the scene to an end.

Finally, there is the concluding scene in which war has been declared. The brothers, dressed in a sequence of insane military costumes, systematically reduce every cliché of every war film ever made to nonsense. In the end, Mrs. Teasdale triumphantly sings the Freedonian national anthem, only to be pelted with loose bits of rubble by the brothers.

Today, *Duck Soup* seems funnier than ever. But when it was released, the movie laid an egg—perhaps because audiences were not in the mood for political satire, perhaps because they did not appreciate having fun made of such serious subjects as patriotism. Whatever the reason, the Marx Brothers' career suffered a slight setback. And though they soon regained the heights, and though their later films had scenes as funny as any they ever made, many of their fans feel they never again were quite the same.

One reason was a change in studios. From Paramount, the Marx Brothers moved to Metro-Goldwyn-Mayer, which had a deserved reputation for producing some of the most stylish and elaborate movies in Hollywood. The problem with the Marx Brothers was that this kind of standard Hollywood production didn't really suit them very well. Their strong point was the systematic destruction of stuffed shirts. Now, in most of their movies, they found themselves surrounded by stuffed shirts who were added to suit the producers of the films. Instead of the Marx Brothers pure, the MGM films had the added attractions of elaborate plots, handsome leading men, beautiful heroines, musical numbers that went on (apparently) forever, and the like, all of which merely slowed the pace of the films and subtracted from the real fun.

In addition, the quality of writing for the Marx Brothers films began to suffer. While the brothers' best fun always seemed to be unorganized and spontaneous, they actually had the services of some of the best comic writers of the time, including S. J. Perelman, George S. Kaufman, and Morris Ryskind. These writers, who could handle every nuance of language with ease, made it possible for the Marx Brothers to go around demolishing every convention but somehow stay within the limits of respectability. At MGM, however, respectability came first. Gradually, the Marx Brothers' wit became less barbed and their gags became more calculated and less spontaneous, and the dull spots in their movies seemed to get longer and longer.

This isn't to say that the later Marx Brothers movies are total disasters; they still had (and have) plenty of fun in them. Indeed, there are some fans who say that *A Night at the Opera*, the brothers' first film for MGM, is the best they ever made.

A Night at the Opera.
Groucho is berated by Sig Rumann, while Chico and Harpo peep
out between them. Margaret Dumont, stately as ever, is at the right.
(*MGM, 1935*)

The plot has Groucho, playing a seedy character named Otis B. Driftwood, promising to introduce a rich social-climbing lady, Mrs. Claypool (Margaret Dumont, of course), to the right people by having her sponsor opera performances. He starts off in the opening scene by leaving Mrs. Claypool alone at a table while he eats dinner with a beautiful blonde. ("Nine dollars and forty cents!" says Groucho when he gets the check. "This is an outrage. If I were you, I wouldn't pay it.") Groucho's efforts to sign up a leading Italian tenor are just as absurd, as he runs into Chico, who is the unscrupulous representative of an aspiring young American tenor.

There follows one of their best scenes, as the two try to negotiate a contract. As Groucho goes through the contract, clause after clause is ripped off and thrown away ("You must have been out on a tear last night," Groucho comments), including a clause that says the contract will be canceled if any of the parties are not in their right mind. ("That's what they call a sanity clause," explains Groucho. "Oh, no, you can't fool me," says Chico. "There ain't no sanity clause." Out it goes.)

As the assorted party sets sail for New York on an ocean liner, Groucho finds that he is in a closet-sized room, made even more crowded by two stowaways who arrive in a trunk. Guess who. The stowaways are followed by a steward, two maids, an engineer, a manicurist, the engineer's assistant, a girl, a charwoman, and assorted more stewards, filling the room to bursting in one of the brothers' most celebrated scenes. It ends when Mrs. Claypool opens the door and is buried under an avalanche of bodies from the room. The movie eventually builds to a climactic scene where the brothers disrupt an opera performance to win the day for the young tenor—not that anyone really cares about him, but the plot calls for it.

The brothers' next film, *A Day at the Races,* is a distinct step down. It is cluttered with awkward musical numbers and marred by some stereotyped racial humor that is painful to watch today. But the film still has its moments as Groucho, playing a horse doctor named Hugo Hackenbush, tries to bluff his way through after being hired to run a sanatorium owned by Margaret Dumont. The moment when Dr. Hackenbush produces a horse pill for Margaret Dumont to swallow, explaining to a skeptical doctor that "The last patient I gave one of those to won the Kentucky Derby" is as good as anything he ever did. And the "Tootsie-Fruitsie ice cream" scene, where Chico, as an ice cream vendor, who is really a race tout, sells Groucho (a) a tip on a race, (b) a code book to read the tipsheet, (c) a master code book to read the code book, (d) a breeders' guide to read the master code book, and (e) yet another book to decipher the breeders' guide is equally inspired nonsense.

There are other scenes to list—the brothers destroying a room at the sanatorium, Chico and Harpo breaking up a date between Groucho and a conniving blonde. (Harpo enters as a detective brandishing a magnifying glass, to be told by Groucho, "If you're looking for my fingerprints, you're a little early.") But something has gone from the relatively pure madness of the early films.

The same is true of the next movie, *At the Circus,* which is one of the Marx Brothers' weaker efforts, even though Groucho does get to sing one of his funniest songs, "Lydia, the Tattooed Lady." The film that follows, *Go West,* never lives up to the opening scene when Groucho, entering a railroad station followed by a crowd of porters, asks them "Any of you boys have change of ten cents?" and, hearing that they don't, replies, "Well, keep the baggage." *The Big Store,* their next effort, is marred by a madcap chase through a department store that is obviously done by stunt men disguised as the brothers.

For all practical purposes, *The Big Store* ended the Marx Brothers' movie career. They appeared together on film twice more, in *A Night in Casablanca,* released in 1946, and *Love Happy,* released in 1949. Both films were only faded reflections of the Marx Brothers at their best, although there are a few moments in each when the old magic returns. Groucho, Harpo, and Chico later appeared individually in movies and on television, but the great days were over.

Chico died in 1961, and Harpo died in 1964. Groucho lived on to become a star on his own television show. In his old age he has been hailed as one of the funniest men who ever lived, giving examples of his quick wit in stage and television appearances when well over eighty. Those who doubted that acclamation were lucky enough to have the old movies still around for anyone to see, movies that are as funny now as they were in the first days when they were released. Decades after they stopped making films, the Marx Brothers can still fill a theater with roars of laughter.

Groucho: I wish to announce that a buffet supper will be served in the next room in five minutes. In order to get you in that room quickly, Mrs. Schmallhausen will sing a soprano solo in this room.

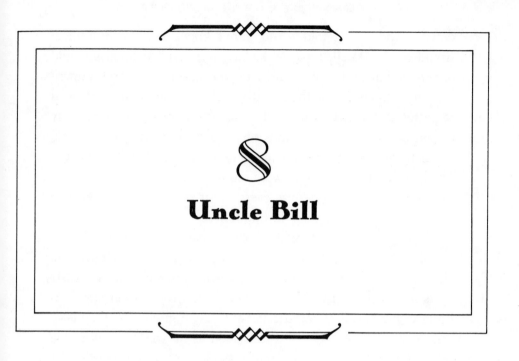

8

Uncle Bill

He was born with the name of William Claude Dukenfield in Philadelphia. He ran away from home at the age of eleven after an argument with his father. He lived as a tramp for years, painfully training himself to become a juggler. He reached the top of his profession in vaudeville after experiencing every hard knock that could be imagined. Rather late in life, he came to the screen to build another career as one of the most unusual comics on film. He was W. C. Fields, the one and only.

It isn't just the bulbous nose and the raffish top hat. It isn't just the voice, which can be mistaken for no other, a voice whose nasal drawl is still being imitated by lesser comedians everywhere. It's everything else—the unique film character that is truly a reflection of the unbelievable real-life W. C. Fields.

Who else, asked how he liked children, would reply with a single sardonic word: "Broiled."? Who else would ask a bartender, "You remember the time I knocked Chicago Molly down?" and, being told, "You didn't knock her down—I did," would reply: "Well, I started kicking her first." Who else would dare to build most of his humor on the nastiness of such American institutions as mothers, little girls, old men, doctors, and respectable businessmen? Who else could be so completely dishonest, so completely unworthy, so completely an old soak, so completely illogical—and make us laugh at it? Who else but Uncle Bill (as his friends were wont to call him) could create his own comic world despite every effort of the most respectable Hollywood executives to hold him down?

Hollywood never really knew what to do with W. C. Fields—which is understandable, since the real world never really knew what to do with him. Possibly because of the early years in which he lived by the skin of his teeth, often cold and hungry, but possibly because he was just himself, W. C. Fields was as much a character off the screen as he was in movies. He had a respect for the dollar that was close to miserliness; in his later, successful years, when Fields signed a contract for $5,000 a week, he insisted that it be paid in cash and on a set schedule —$2,500 on Monday, $2,500 on Wednesday. Having once been caught in a stock market loss, he got the habit of opening bank accounts in any place he happened to be—and he was in quite a few places during a long career. Some of the accounts were opened in his own name, some were opened in the outlandish names that later became his delight, and many went ignored forever.

It should be said that W. C. Fields had about every fault known to the human race, including jealousy, intemperance, intolerance, miserliness, and mysogyny. It should also be said that he has collected a band of fans as dedicated as any that ever existed, and that the author of this book is one of them. Some people never get to like W. C. Fields. Some become addicted to him. And those who are Fields addicts find that, contrary to the usual rule of watching comedies, Fields films get better on repetition.

Some fans have seen *The Bank Dick, Never Give a Sucker an Even Break,* or other Fields classics twenty or more times, each time finding some small new bit of business that sets them laughing as hard as ever. Once hooked on Fields, a movie viewer is hooked for good.

If one needs a reason for forgiving Fields his faults, it could be found in the fact that the world was a very hard place for him during the years when most people are enjoying a happy childhood. Too stubborn to return to his family after running away, Fields had to live by his wits, which sometimes meant working but often meant something shadier. Somehow, he got the idea of becoming a juggler and, in the midst of this chaos, he trained himself to be one of the best jugglers the world has ever seen. Make no mistake, it wasn't easy; Fields worked for hours, driving himself until he had mastered his skill in spite of all the real physical pain and discouragement he encountered. His love of money, his distrust of other people, and his drinking (to relax his nerves, frayed after such mental and physical effort) could all be traced back to these early years.

In the long run, it paid off; after the expected hard knocks, Fields became one of the highest-paid stars of vaudeville and went on to star on Broadway in the Ziegfeld Follies. After proving himself as a juggler, he had just as hard a time proving that he could be a comedian, but he did that too, starring in several stage successes.

Fields entered films during the silent days, but his real success came after the movies learned to talk. Even so, most of his early films had him merely as comic relief, someone who made a brief appearance to dress up a standard plot. However, even in the early days he was making films that now are recognized as classics.

One such film is *It's a Gift,* in which Fields plays the harried owner of a small-town general store who inherits a run-down orange grove in California and, in spite of all odds, ends up wealthy and happy. Scene after scene is a classic: Fields's store being demolished by the combined efforts of a sweet young tot and a blind old man; Fields trying to get to sleep in spite of every possible obstacle, including a vegetable man shouting his wares, a collapsing porch swing, two noisy women, and a ball bouncing loudly downstairs; Fields talking to the unscrupulous agent who is trying to buy his orange grove. ("You're drunk," says the agent. "You're crazy," says Fields, adding after a moment: "I'll be sober tomorrow, but you'll be crazy for the rest of your life.")

So are the handful of shorts that Fields made—films that were almost ignored at the time, but which are treasured now. It is hard to pick a favorite, but most Fields fans have a warm spot for *The Fatal Glass of Beer*, a film set in the frozen north and built loosely around a plot that has Fields and his movie wife greeting a son who is coming home after a spell in prison for stealing bonds.

Only a true Fields fan can double up at such dead-pan lines as "I think I'll go out and milk the elk." But, with a little training, almost anyone can appreciate Fields, still wearing mittens, strumming the dulcimer to sing a tuneless, non-rhyming song about the glass of beer that sent his son to his doom, or Fields stepping periodically to the door of his cabin to say, "And it ain't a fit night out for man or beast," and to have a fistful of fake snow thrown in his face. The fact that the son gets thrown out in the snow at the end of the film because his parents are disappointed to learn that he didn't steal the bonds is only to be expected.

Probably the best of Fields is in the last four full-length films he made. By this time, Fields had gotten into the habit of selling movie studios outrageous plots, often scrawled on the backs of envelopes and attributed to unbelievable authors (Mahatma Kane Jeeves, or Otis Cribblecoblis, for instance), for any price he cared to mention. The plot hardly mattered, because

Fields would merely go out and be himself in front of the camera, which was usually more than enough to make the film a success.

You Can't Cheat an Honest Man, made in 1939, had Fields playing Larson E. Whipsnade, the owner of a bankrupt circus that is always just one jump ahead of its creditors. Also in the film are ventriloquist Edgar Bergen and his dummy, Charley McCarthy, with whom Fields had a long feud, especially on radio shows. Audiences today will sit patiently through the occasionally funny bits by Bergen to see such sights as Fields short-changing two dishonest customers at the ticket window and Fields breaking up a society party by constantly mentioning snakes in the presence of a woman who faints every time they are mentioned.

The next movie, *My Little Chickadee,* starred Fields alongside Mae West, who had made a career out of being a female W. C. Fields. *My Little Chickadee* had a plot that could be detected by someone who looked hard enough, but by and large the two stars just made it up as they went along. The results were not as good as their fans had expected, since Fields and Miss West spent a lot of effort at trying to top each other. But some of their exchanges are priceless—for example, when a man asks Fields at the start of a poker game, "Is this a game of chance?" and he answers, "Not the way I play it."

But the film that followed *My Little Chickadee* was Fields at his best. *The Bank Dick,* released in 1940, is regarded by most of Uncle Bill's fans as the best movie he ever made and one of the enduring comic classics of the screen. Fields had a free hand in writing and making the film, and the result is a frolic that only Fields could produce. In the film, Fields plays a character named Egbert Sousè, a name that everyone insists on pronouncing souse (as in drunk), only to be told solemnly by Fields that there is "an accent grave over the E." Sousè has a nagging mother-in-law, an unsympathetic wife, and a brat of a

My Little Chickadee.
W. C. Fields is about to betroth Mae West in one of the oddest film romances ever recorded. (*Universal, 1940*)

W. C. Fields.
The Great Man demonstrates one of his many talents to an admiring
crowd in *The Bank Dick*. (*Universal, 1941*)

daughter; he is given to embroidering the truth, has no visible source of income, and spends most of his time in a raffish joint named the Black Pussy Cafe. Yet this totally unworthy hero is a rich man at the end of the film. He captures a pair of bank holdup men by sheer accident (getting a job as bank dick in the process), bluffs his way into a position as movie director, sells a worthless story to the movies for $10,000, and buys (with embezzled money) shares in a worthless gold mine that eventually is found to have real gold in it.

It is hopeless to make sense out of *The Bank Dick*, so the best thing to do is relax and enjoy it. There is plenty to enjoy: Fields as a movie director, explaining to an actor in full evening dress and top hat that the film now will have a football scene in it, and the hero will score "touchdown after touchdown." "In these clothes?" asks the hero acidly. "Well, maybe we could change the hat," Fields replies. There is Fields coming into the Black Pussy Cafe to ask, "Say, was I in here last night, and did I spend a twenty-dollar bill?" "Yes," is the answer, and Fields says, "Thank goodness. I thought I lost it." And there is a little boy, pointing to Fields's bulbous nose, who is told by his mother, "Never mind, Willie, you'd like to have a nose like that full of nickels."

The Bank Dick is a movie full of sight gags and throwaway lines, some of which make sense only to Fields and some of which become funny only on the fourth or fifth hearing. Dedicated Fields fans regard the film as pure gold from start to finish and they never miss a chance to see it, which isn't a bad idea at all.

But Fields's next film also ranks high with his fans, even though it has a serious claim to being called one of the worst, most disorganized movies ever made. But that is exactly what Fields intended. He started by giving it an impossible title, *Never Give a Sucker an Even Break* (explaining to a friend

78

that he expected it would appear on movie marquees as "W. C. Fields—*Sucker*") and then gave it an even more impossible plot (for which he was paid his usual $25,000).

Never Give a Sucker an Even Break stars Fields as a movie star who is disliked by the head of the studio (played by Franklin Pangborn, one of Fields's favorite supporting actors, who also appeared in *The Bank Dick* as J. Pinkerton Snoopington, a bank examiner), who is unrecognized by his fans, and who is insulted by waitresses in cheap diners. After meandering about for a while, the film appears to get down to business as Fields tries to sell a movie plot to the studio head.

But what a plot! Among other fantastic twists, it has Fields flying in an airplane with an open observation deck. When his bottle falls over the side, Fields jumps after it. He lands on a mountaintop inhabited by a pet gorilla, a stately dowager named Mrs. Hemoglobin (played by Margaret Dumont), and her pretty blond daughter. After a kissing game with the daughter and an effort to marry the rich mother, Fields wanders to a country named Russia where many of the inhabitants are dressed in Mexican costumes. Eventually, the film returns to "real life," where Fields is fired for proposing such a bad script. Then comes a very funny chase scene in which Fields's car is hooked by a fire engine, so that he cannot control it but can be hit by oncoming cars. When the chase ends with the demolition of the car, the film ends, too, just as haphazardly as when it began.

That was about the end of Fields's film career, although he did make an occasional appearance in later years. A lifetime of heavy drinking had taken its toll, and Fields was often ill. He died on Christmas day in 1946. His films are still shown regularly, and they have not dated one bit. W. C. Fields, the reprobate, the irascible, the man who set his own rules and broke all the standard rules, is as funny today as ever.

9

The Screwball Comedies

The 1930s saw the rise of a new sort of movie comedy, films in which the focus switched from the actors to the script writers and directors. With a few exceptions, the great comedians of the early movie days also directed their films; Chaplin, Keaton, and Lloyd, for example, did it all. Even when movies got more complex, requiring a split between actors and directors, many comedies were still essentially the creation of their stars. A Marx Brothers film or a W. C. Fields comedy are so much the product of the performers' skills that hardly anyone but real film buffs can name the director.

But alongside these films there are comedies that are best listed under the directors' names—a Frank Capra film, a Billy Wilder film, a Preston Sturges film. Each of these directors had his favorite actors and favorite writers (a highly important point, since the success of these comedies depended on the wittiness of the dialogue), but there was no question that the film owed its success or failure to the skill of the director, who put everything together and often did as much work on the script as the screen writers who got the credit.

An economic factor outside the movie world played an important part in shaping these comedies. The 1920s had been a time of prosperity. The 1930s were a time of depression, with millions out of work and millions more on the edge of survival. The movies offered one of the few opportunities to escape from the grim reality of the Great Depression into a world that, for a few hours at least, was full of people who were happy and who had all the money they needed.

Thus was born the "screwball comedy" of the 1930s, a film in which the focus was the absurd actions of the rich. For audiences who had no money, these screwball comedies had two attractions—first, the opportunity to bask in luxury for a few hours and, second, the opportunity to see that rich people aren't necessarily smarter than poor people. Indeed, the lesson taught by the films was that the "little guy" was a better guide than the rich man; when working people or the poor appear in these films, they always show up better than the rich, and one of the enduring themes of the films is the triumph of the little guy over the rich and powerful.

That theme was expressed very well in one of the earliest and best of the screwball comedies, *It Happened One Night,* which won just about every Academy Award for 1934. Directed by Frank Capra (who was previously responsible for Harry Langdon's best movies), *It Happened One Night* starred Clark Gable as a tough, wisecracking newspaper reporter and Claudette Colbert as a runaway heiress who wanted to marry a good-for-nothing aviator. She marries the reporter, of course, but only after a series of half-dramatic, half-funny adventures on a bus traveling north from Florida. All along the way, the film contrasts the real, warm life of the poor people on the bus with the phony, high-pressure life of the rich girl. Capra, Gable, and

Colbert won Academy Awards, as did Robert Riskin, who wrote the script, and the film itself was voted best of the year.

Capra followed *It Happened One Night* with a string of successful comedies that taught the same moral. James Stewart was a favorite leading man of these Capra films, the best of which include *Mr. Deeds Goes to Town* (which starred Gary Cooper), *You Can't Take It With You, Mr. Smith Goes to Washington,* and *Meet John Doe.*

The lessons Capra preached in these movies (and he did do some preaching) were always the same: money doesn't buy happiness, wise guys may win part of the time but always lose at the end, the rich and powerful are not to be trusted, and a simple but honest man will triumph against any odds.

The lesson is taught in different ways. In *Mr. Deeds Goes to Town,* Gary Cooper is a down-home boy from Mandrake Falls, Vermont, who inherits $20 million and comes to New York. A hard-boiled woman newspaper reporter played by Jean Arthur (another Capra favorite) worms her way into Mr. Deeds's affections, writes a series of newspaper stories holding him up to ridicule, and breaks his heart. When an out-of-work man breaks into the Deeds mansion with a gun, sobbing because he cannot feed his family, Deeds decides to give away his fortune by buying farms for the poor. The villain, a shrewd lawyer, tries to have Deeds declared insane, and Deeds is so downhearted he does not fight—until he learns that he is loved, which leads to the happy ending.

In *Mr. Smith Goes to Washington,* James Stewart is a simple, down-home boy who is appointed to the United States Senate because the political bosses think he will be easy to handle. A hard-boiled newspaperwoman, played by Jean Arthur, is hired to keep him under control but falls in love with him. Mr. Smith discovers a plot to swindle the public by building an unneeded dam, is accused of being responsible for the swindle, and man-

Mr. Smith Goes to Washington.
Good Guy James Stewart confronts Bad Guy Edward Arnold in the
Frank Capra classic. (*Columbia, 1939*)

ages to expose the real villains at the end with the help of a dramatic filibuster in the Senate Chamber.

In *You Can't Take It With You*, a happy-go-lucky family whose members do exactly as they please in life convert a stuffy rich man to their way of thinking. And in *Meet John Doe*, a down-and-out tramp, who is used by rich men to control public opinion, exposes the villains in the end mostly by the force of his sincerity. All of these films might sound obvious and naïve in our cynical times, but they were exactly in the mood of their era, and Capra was an excellent director who invariably had fine actors and actresses to work with. Despite the passage of the years and the change in the national mood, the great Capra films of the 1930s are still as funny—and as moving—as they were when they were first made.

A director who did not have Capra's sentimental streak was Howard Hawks, who zigzagged between making action dramas (*The Dawn Patrol, Scarface*) and some of the best comedies of the time. Hawks was responsible for *Bringing Up Baby*, which has a claim to being the best screwball comedy of them all. *Bringing Up Baby* has Cary Grant as an absent-minded scientist, Katharine Hepburn as the society girl who falls in love with him at first sight, and a leopard named Baby who helps considerably to keep the plot moving. Hawks's trademark was crackling, fast dialogue (he always had his characters speak a little faster than normal) and nonstop plot development; not much of *Bringing Up Baby* makes sense in retrospect, but the film is too funny to analyze while the action is zipping along. The plot is sufficiently described by saying that Hepburn gets Grant and Grant gets the million-dollar gift for his museum, while Baby gets a happy home. (Nearly thirty years later, Peter Bogdanovich borrowed the framework of the plot and Hawks's style to make *What's Up, Doc?* which starred Ryan O'Neal and Barbra Streisand and had plenty of funny moments, although it never reached the level of the older film.)

Hawks also made *Twentieth Century,* which starred John Barrymore as a temperamental Broadway director and Carole Lombard as an unknown who is turned into a star by Barrymore, learns to hate him, learns to love him, and ends back under his thumb. *His Girl Friday,* a Hawks screen version of the Broadway hit *Front Page,* has Cary Grant as a tough, unscrupulous Chicago newspaper editor and Rosalind Russell as his star reporter who is leaving the newspaper for marriage and a more normal life. *Ball of Fire* has Gary Cooper as a dreamy professor who is captured by a burlesque queen, played by Barbara Stanwyck. In all of these films, the plot moves like lightning, any person or institution of dignity is fair game, and the laughs come one after another.

Gooier films were made by Leo McCarey, a director who broke in with Hal Roach (he directed some Laurel and Hardy shorts) and eventually was to make some highly successful films in which Bing Crosby and Barry Fitzgerald played Catholic priests. McCarey's best comedy of the 1930s was *The Awful Truth,* which won an Academy Award in 1937 and starred Cary Grant and Irene Dunne as a married couple who became divorced but eventually, after a number of adventures, realized they were still in love. Other McCarey films worth remembering include *Ruggles of Red Gap,* which had Charles Laughton as a proper British butler exposed to the American wild West, and *Six of a Kind,* whose cast included W. C. Fields.

One master whose films have slipped somewhat from sight today—perhaps because his career faded badly at the end, perhaps because he was almost completely unsentimental—is Preston Sturges. He came along rather late in the history of the screwball comedy. His first film, *The Great McGinty,* was made in 1940, and by 1949 he was dropped by Hollywood. But in between came a string of comedies with ingenuous plots and marvelous dialogue, much of it written by Sturges.

The Sturges comedies are strong stuff, in which most con-

Bringing Up Baby.
Cary Grant on the left, Katharine Hepburn on the right, and Baby, the leopard, in the middle. (*RKO, 1938*)

The Great McGinty.
Brian Donlevy, who plays McGinty (right), is having a slight dispute with Akim Tamiroff. (*Paramount, 1940*)

ventional ideas are turned upside down. *The Great McGinty*, for example, is the cynical saga of a bum (played by Brian Donlevy) who enters politics by selling his vote for $2.00 (thirty-seven times in the same election!), fights his way to the top by sheer crookedness, and is ruined only when he decides to turn honest.

Sullivan's Travels is about a successful Hollywood director of comedies who wants to make films of "social significance," and who disguises himself as a tramp to see "real life." Through a bizarre accident, Sullivan becomes a convict and learns that making people laugh is socially significant.

The Lady Eve is about a rich young fool (Henry Fonda) who falls in love with a wise young woman card sharp (Barbara Stanwyck), walks out on her when he finds out she is a swindler, and eventually is taught a lesson by the young lady (who gets her man).

Sentiment sneaks into some Sturges comedies. *Hail the Conquering Hero* plays Eddie Bracken as the son of a World War I hero who enlists in the marines but is discharged because he has hay fever. Eddie has a friend send letters back from the Pacific to make his mother believe that he is a hero, but he is afraid to go home and face the truth. A band of marines pick him up, give him a uniform, and provide a moment of glory that gets carried too far. In the end, Eddie confesses to the whole town and is elected mayor, in a scene that is genuinely touching.

Sturges's movies seemed to have dropped out of sight in recent years, perhaps because his touch deserted him early, while other directors of his era are still active. But they do come around, on television or in some revival theaters, from time to time. If you get a chance to see one of Sturges's comedies, grab it.

Aside from Sturges's films, screwball comedies went out

Some Like It Hot.
Jack Lemmon and Tony Curtis, disguised to escape gangsters, play their hearts out. (*United Artists, 1959*)

of style in the 1940s. The main reason was the war, which not only made everyone think about battlefields and production lines but also brought back prosperity. Whatever the reasons, the light touch of the 1930s just about vanished. One exception, however, was a director who carries on the tradition (with some modification) to this day—Billy Wilder, who was born in Austria, made a name for himself in Hollywood, and then went on to become one of our finest directors.

Wilder has made a number of excellent comedies, but his best seems to be *Some Like It Hot,* made in 1959, which starred Jack Lemmon and Tony Curtis as two Chicago musicians who saw a gangland massacre and were forced to flee to Florida disguised as women, because the only jobs available are in an all-girl band. In Florida, Tony Curtis sets out in pursuit of Sugar Cane, played by the one and only Marilyn Monroe, while Jack Lemmon finds himself pursued by an aging millionaire. The gangsters who staged the Chicago massacre show up at the Florida resort, spot the boys at a gangland banquet that features the rub out of one mob chief, and set off on a chase of the heroes. Curtis gets Marilyn Monroe and Lemmon is gotten by the millionaire, whose response when he learns that Lemmon is a man is priceless: "Well, no one's perfect."

Funny though it is, the film is full of violence and hard truths, which is true of most of Wilder's comedies, e.g., *The Fortune Cookie,* which centers around the efforts of a scheming shyster lawyer to cheat an insurance company by using an injury suffered by his brother-in-law (Walter Matthau plays the lawyer, Jack Lemmon the injured man); *One, Two, Three,* which manages to be hilariously funny about two very unfunny things, postwar Germany and the Russian occupation of Berlin; and so on. It is a long way from the cheerful innocence of Frank Capra's comedies to the world of Billy Wilder, which is a hard place to get along in.

Maybe that's why the screwball comedy has vanished: the world has become a place where it is harder and harder to laugh innocently about things like love and poverty and wealth. It's hard to think of a dreary time like the Great Depression as the "good old days"; millions were out of work and many were actually starving. But if you think of all the great talents working then, they were the good old days of movie comedy.

10

Selected Short Subjects

People who shelled out hard-earned money to go to the movies in the 1930s and 1940s expected their money's worth, and got it. The usual fare at your neighborhood theater was a double feature (two films, one a major production and one a run-of-the-mill mystery or Western) plus a newsreel plus, most of the time, a short subject that ran for two reels, or twenty minutes. (Sometimes the theater gave away dishes too, but that's another story.) As a result, Hollywood was busy as it could never be now, grinding out films to meet what seemed like an endless demand. And many of those films were comedy short subjects, which quickly became a world of their own.

You could see almost anyone in a short: people on the way down (Harry Langdon, Buster Keaton, and Mack Sennett made shorts), people on the way up (Bing Crosby, among others, made his first movie appearances in Mack Sennett two-reelers), sometimes a great star like W. C. Fields. But many of the shorts were made by comics who did nothing else, working under directors who specialized in shorts. Considering that quantity, not quality, was the main concern most of the time, it isn't surprising that most of these shorts have been forgotten quickly. What is surprising is that many of them have endured, and that some of them are still being shown in movie theaters and on television to this day. If you're a weekend television viewer, you may have seen some of these shorts yourself.

Take the Three Stooges, who set an unmatched record of durability. The Stooges made their first movie short early in the 1930s. They kept on making films until 1958, and by that time they had about 200 two-reelers to their credit. The critics, to say the least, never liked the Three Stooges. The public obviously did—and still does, because their films are being shown on many television stations. The Stooges obviously had every fault imaginable, from bad taste to bad plots. But they had the magic knack of making people laugh, and that was enough to ignite a lasting career in short subjects.

No one ever accused the Three Stooges of being subtle. In fact, if you wanted to be unkind about this funny trio, you could say that their stocks in trade were incompetence and brutality. The Three Stooges were forever showing up in places where they had no right to be (when the time came to invent a plot, they would ask themselves, "Where would we be most out of place?"), and they would make all the obvious mistakes— imagine the Three Stooges as plumbers!

In the course of committing their blunders, they would poke fingers in each other's eyes, hit each other over the head with hammers, slam each other across the stomach with ladders, drop anvils on each other's toes, and do whatever other violence was possible within the limitations of their plot. Put in so many words, it sounds very mechanical, but the Stooges had a way of making audiences laugh at the obvious that has not vanished even in these sophisticated days.

One problem in trying to trace the history of the Three Stooges is that there were more than three of them. The act started as Ted Healy and His Stooges in vaudeville. Ted Healy was a popular comic of the 1920s, and his Stooges were Moe Howard (the one with the over-the-eyes hairdo who provides whatever brainpower the trio possesses), Larry Fine (he's the one with the crazy hairdo), and Moe's younger brother Jerry, better known as Curly, who played the burly, bald and invincibly rock-headed Stooge around whose antics the act revolved. Moe, Larry, and Curly made a fine team until the 1940s, when Curly had to step out because of illness. His place was taken by Sam Howard, another brother, called "Shemp" in the shorts (sharp eyes can spot him as the bartender in W. C. Fields's *The Bank Dick*), who was later replaced by Joe Besser and, finally, by Joe DeRita. Fans of the Stooges believe that the best of their films were those made with Curly.

The Three Stooges occupy a strange place in the history of the comedy film. Officially, they are deplorable. All of their gags and situations are predictable and, often, are in bad taste. Everything they did was done, and better, at one time or another by other comedy teams. The plots for many of their shorts are almost nonexistent; the Stooges would more or less invent many plots as they went along. Their humor is usually low, dumb, and obvious. All you can say in their favor is that they could keep audiences laughing, and that is something that cannot be said for many would-be comedians who had more intelligence, better taste, and better plots than the Three Stooges ever did.

The Three Stooges never wanted to win an Academy Award (although one of their shorts was nominated for an Oscar) or astonish intellectuals. They just wanted to make a lot of money by being funny. They managed to do exactly that, building a career that lasted longer than most other movie careers. In their own way, they kept alive the great slapstick tradition that

The Three Stooges.
Having their usual difficulties, this time as music makers in *Snow White and the Three Stooges,* one of their full-length films. (*20th Century-Fox, 1961*)

was established by Mack Sennett. With all their faults, the Three Stooges need not apologize for themselves. They did what they set out to do, and people are still laughing because of them.

If you ever watch a Three Stooges comedy, you may notice that they have a gift given to few comedians—they are able to carry a picture, however ridiculous, along by the sheer force of their personalities. Ignore the eye-gouging and the phony sound effects, concentrate on that special gift, and you will be able to understand why the Stooges lasted as long as they did, and why their films still are shown. Even after their contract to do shorts ended, the Stooges still had enough of a following to do full-length features (*The Three Stooges Meet Hercules, Snow White and the Three Stooges,* among others), which are funny in their own way. Such endurance—some three decades of filmmaking—is almost unmatched among film comedians, and it is the Three Stooges's ultimate monument.

A comedy group that proved to be nearly as durable as the Three Stooges, but with a totally different style, was Our Gang, which was starred in more than a hundred shorts over a twenty-two-year period. Our Gang can be described simply: it was a bunch of kids having good, clean fun. The actors portraying those kids changed as time went by (that had to be, because child actors grow up), directors and writers came and went, but the basic idea survived for two decades.

Indeed, it survives today, for the Our Gang comedies are still being shown on many television stations as "The Little Rascals." The fact that these comedies, made so long ago in a country that has changed so much over the years, can still hold a television audience, says a lot about the worth of the Our Gang series.

No one ever claimed that the Our Gang comedies were classics that could rank with Chaplin and Keaton. But they did something that few films have ever done—they captured the special magic of childhood. Our Gang is not a collection of pampered child actors putting on a special show. It is a neighborhood gang of kids having fun in the way that kids have always had fun—putting on shows, getting in trouble with the teacher, doing all the things that kids do. Sure, it's all done in an exaggerated way for the movies, but there is enough truth at the core of Our Gang to make the appeal of the series much more durable than anyone could have anticipated.

Not many people who are around today have seen the original Our Gang, which originated in 1922 at the Hal Roach studio. It started with a young black actor named Ernie Morrison, who gave Hal Roach the idea of a series built around children; added to the first Our Gang were Mary Kornman, Jackie Davis, Allen Clayton Hoskins (who became famous as Farina), Jackie Condon, Mickey Daniels, and Joe Cobb. The series was a hit from the start, and one reason was the care that was taken to recruit the members of Our Gang. Hal Roach did not want the typical spoiled brats who run after a movie career. He wanted children who could act like real children, and he got them. Although everything they did was put on film, the secret of Our Gang's success was that, at heart, they did not act the way Hollywood stars would act.

And one other thing has to be said. Our Gang was far ahead of its times in its handling of racial humor—because most of the time there was no racial humor. The group always included a black child (the best known is Billy "Buckwheat" Thomas), but it was unusual to have the black child lapse into the eye-rolling, crap-shooting stereotype of Negro humor. Most of the time, Buckwheat was just another member of Our Gang, one of the kids on the block—a highly unusual situation in an era when racial segregation was the rule. It took three decades and more for the rest of the nation to catch up to Our Gang and learn that black kids are just kids like anyone else.

The Our Gang group that television viewers are accustomed to seeing is the bunch that flourished in the 1930s. They

Our Gang.
The entire troupe lines up for fire drill in *Watch My Smoke,* one
of the gang's early efforts. (*Roach-MGM*)

include Jackie Cooper (who left the group after a few years to achieve stardom on his own), Carl (Alfalfa) Sweitzer, Buckwheat, Mary Ann Jackson, Norman Chaney (who played the fat boy), Dorothy De Borba, Bobby (Wheezer) Hutchins, Scotty Beckett, and Spanky McFarland. One adult also has to be mentioned: June Marlowe, the pretty young actress who played Miss Crabtree, Our Gang's teacher.

A lot of fun happened in the introduction of Miss Crabtree (the gang assumed that any schoolteacher with that name had to be dried-up, crabby, and old) and in the course of Jackie Cooper's crush on the pretty teacher. But she wasn't the only adult to appear in the series; if you look close you can see such Hal Roach standbys as Billy Gilbert, Franklin Pangborn (the actor W. C. Fields loved to use), Edgar Kennedy, and James Finlayson (who appeared in so many Laurel and Hardy films). The directors changed from time to time. Robert McGowan started the series, giving way in the 1930s to Gus Meins, whose films are regarded as the best of the lot. Gordon Douglas took over as director later, to be followed by Edward Cahn and others.

Somewhere along the line the fun began to wear thin, mostly because the people making the Our Gang films lost sight of the reasons why the series had become so popular. Instead of being just ordinary kids, the gang, under the direction of adults who thought they were being wise, began to get slicker and slicker. Music was added to the shorts, which was a good idea at first. The *Our Gang Follies*, named after the year they were made, worked out fine at first, but the musical numbers in these films got too elaborate after a while. Then the shorts were cut from two reels to one, giving almost no time to develop character. By the 1940s, the Our Gang comedies were strictly production-line efforts, with none of the free-and-easy attitude that had been the rule at the start.

MGM, which had taken over the series from Hal Roach, stopped production in 1944. As early as 1950, the films were being shown on television. They still are being shown in many cities, and some of them now have been seen by three generations of youngsters. There were a few halfhearted attempts to revive Our Gang, but none of them succeeded, and it is highly unlikely that any such group could succeed today. They were made in an era when children were innocent, and that era is over. Life is very different today, and laughs don't come as easily as they once did. But we still have Our Gang around to remind us of the way things used to be.

But if the childhood antics of the 1930s and 1940s still can be appreciated, the same cannot be said of the grown-up comedies of the time. The Edgar Kennedy shorts are an example. They were just as popular as the Our Gang comedies for nearly as long (they were made from 1931 to 1948) but they rarely are seen today, even though Edgar Kennedy was a grown-up version of Our Gang.

Our Gang consisted of ordinary kids; Edgar Kennedy was the average American, running into the average American problems. Kennedy had a nagging mother-in-law, an obnoxious brother-in-law, and a wife (usually played by Florence Lake) who caused trouble in spite of herself. None of it was memorable trouble, but just the kind of problems that anyone might run into. Kennedy tried to lose weight, tried to start a balky outboard motor to go fishing, tried to bottle fruit preserves to save money, tried to do all the things that any homeowner would do—but always with disastrous results.

Kennedy was not one of the world's greatest clowns, but he was an experienced comic who had played alongside many of the best comedians of the time at the Hal Roach studio. He was a large, burly, bald-headed man who had a trade-mark; when anything particularly distressing happened, he would put his hand at his forehead and wipe it slowly down across his face to disclose a look of immense disgust. (If you see *Duck Soup,* you might recognize Edgar Kennedy as the peanut vendor who has a losing encounter with Harpo.) And for the record, Kennedy had the good fortune to be directed by some outstanding talents, including Hal Yates and George Stevens, who later went on to fame in such films as *Shane.* But Kennedy's shorts, for all their virtues, are hardly ever seen today.

The same is true of the nearly 100 comedy shorts made by another funny man, Leon Errol. He was short and bald, usually a little tipsy (which gave him the chance to show off his most celebrated trick, the wobbly "rubber legs" that sent him in every which direction), and a master of all the standard vaudeville tricks of the trade. His shorts, which generally featured Errol as a married man who was in trouble with his wife because of involvement with a pretty girl, were so successful that Errol played in a number of feature films, including *Never Give a Sucker an Even Break.* His career was going strong until his death from a heart attack in 1951.

There were many other successful series of short subjects. Noteworthy among them were the Pete Smith comedies, which had Smith narrating while a stuntman named Dave O'Brien experienced various disasters on the screen, and the comedies that brought Robert Benchley, one of America's best humorists, to the screen to deliver a series of lectures on such subjects as *How to Train a Dog* and *How to Be a Detective.* All of these live on in memory, but few of them can be seen outside museums devoted to old films.

Television killed the short subjects. Not only did television draw people away from the movies, so that the double feature with selected short subjects died a quick death, but television also produced a natural replacement for the short subject—the half-hour television series. The short subject and the

Edgar Kennedy.
In a placid but suspicious mood in the short *Rags to Riches*. At left, smirking, is Jack Oakie, another funny man of the era. (*Republic, 1941*)

Leon Errol, right.
In *Bested by a Beard*, one of his many film shorts. The dismayed young man is Arthur O'Connell. (*RKO, 1940*)

television situation comedy were so much alike that some of the directors from the movies switched to television without skipping a beat.

The short subjects that now sit in vaults may come back some day, since nostalgia is the style these days. When a new generation sees these films, it will get a chance to recapture the feeling of the days when life was simpler, the movies were free in spirit, and Hollywood was a vast factory that ground out comedies which often were surprisingly good.

11

A Gaggle of Gagmen

There have been many funny men of the movies who can't easily be put in a neat category. There are many ways of getting laughs, from baggy-pants burlesque antics to Keystone Kops slapstick to sophisticated drawing-room comedy. A "typical" screen comedian simply cannot be described, because there is no such thing.

Alec Guinness, for example, is clearly one of the great actors of our time. He was knighted by Queen Elizabeth II for his achievements. Yet Guinness first appeared on the American screen as the hero of a series of British comedies in the years after World War II, and those comedies showed that Guinness could be as funny as anyone who ever made a film.

It came as a great surprise to many Americans to learn that the British could make comedies that were truly comic. For decades, Americans had been telling themselves that the British were a dull, solemn people with a paralyzed sense of humor.

Alec Guinness.
Facing the outraged captains of industry in one of his best films,
Man in the White Suit. (Ealing, 1951)

The postwar comedies killed that idea. True, some of the British accents were difficult to understand and some of the jokes were peculiarly British. But still, the basic situations and the skills of actors, directors, and producers were enough to make comedies that anyone could appreciate. Guinness wasn't in all of those comedies, but he was in some of the best.

It's hard to pick a favorite, but a good picture to start with is *Kind Hearts and Coronets,* in which Guinness plays eight different roles. The plot doesn't sound very funny (it's about a young man who becomes a duke by methodically murdering every other member of the family) but the film is very funny indeed. Guinness plays everyone who is murdered—a general, an admiral, a suffragette, a gay young blade, and so on. His ability to act such varying roles with such impeccable style showed Guinness at his best. (It should be mentioned that the film ends with a twist, so that the debonair murderer is brought to justice.)

In *The Man in the White Suit,* Guinness plays an eccentric young scientist who brings both unions and management in the textile industry into turmoil by inventing a fabric that never gets dirty and never wears out. He shares honors in the film with the musical score, a marvelous collection of burblings and gurgles that go with Guinness' chemical apparatus. In *The Lavender Hill Mob,* Guinness is a timid clerk at the Bank of England who masterminds a million-pound gold theft. In *The Captain's Paradise,* Guinness plays the skipper of a ferry that shuttles between Gibraltar and Africa; he has a wife in each port, and the film shows the inevitable disaster of that situation.

There are more Guinness comedies, but those are enough to prove the point: Alec Guinness is a very funny man. Guinness made a few weak films (who hasn't?) but most of his movies are well worth seeing whenever they appear on television or in a revival theater.

At the other end of the comedy spectrum from Alec Guinness are Bud Abbott and Lou Costello, who starred in comedies that were anything but subtle and witty. Abbott and Costello have one distinction: they are probably the last movie stars to emerge from the rowdy world of burlesque. Abbott (the tall, thin straight man) and Costello (the little, round comic) had been knocking around in burlesque and the movies with no great distinction for years, until they were starred in a low-cost comedy titled *Buck Privates* in 1941. The United States was uneasily preparing for war, and the nation was ready for a comedy about two schnooks who enlist in the Army by accident. The picture is mostly an excuse for Abbott and Costello to do a long string of comedy routines of the kind that were successful with generations of burlesque fans, but the pair had excellent timing and delivery; movie audiences laughed as loudly as burlesque audiences once had, and *Buck Privates* was a surprising box-office smash.

Universal, which had Abbott and Costello under contract, rushed three more of their movies into distribution by the end of 1941. *In the Navy* was a logical sequel, with the comics as blundering sailors rather than blundering soldiers. *Hold That Ghost* got its laughs from putting Abbott and Costello into a haunted house for all the predictable scare scenes. *Keep 'Em Flying* had all the airplane jokes that could be expected.

Abbott and Costello kept on making movies for several years, but the comedies that followed in the later 1940s were usually not as good as the pair's first few screen hits. The reason was simple: Abbott and Costello became a hit because they were very good at delivering tried-and-true vaudeville and burlesque gag lines and routines. They never created a character in the way that Keaton or Fields did; they were always just two comics going through routines. Once they used up the backlog of routines, the boys began to slide. However, almost every film has at least one good routine, which is worth waiting for.

The best routine of all is "Who's on First," in which Abbott drives Costello crazy by talking about a baseball team that

Abbott and Costello.
Lou Costello is out on a limb and Bud Abbott offers support in
Keep 'Em Flying, one of their early films. (*Universal, 1941*)

Road to Morocco.
Bing Crosby, Dorothy Lamour, and Bob Hope in one of the Road
films that they turned out for Paramount. (*Paramount, 1942*)

has Who on first, What on second, I Don't Know on third, and the like. The routine had been done by Abbott and Costello on radio, on the stage and everywhere else (there is now a recording of it in the Baseball Hall of Fame), and it became their trade-mark. For the record, the film in which "Who's on First" was done was *Naughty Nineties,* which has almost nothing else to recommend it and which is almost never seen today.

After a while, the films were as predictable as the titles indicate: *Abbott and Costello Meet Frankenstein, Abbott and Costello in the Foreign Legion, Abbott and Costello Meet the Mummy.* By the mid-1950s, the pair's film career was just about over. A television series did not last long, and Abbott and Costello split in 1957. Attempts to make it on their own failed, and the Abbott and Costello story was over. They never won an Academy Award or got much credit from the critics, but they did make a lot of people laugh at one time or another, and that was all they wanted to do.

The brief rise and fall of Abbott and Costello contrasts with the success story of Bob Hope, whose movie career has lasted more than thirty years and has helped make him a fortune. Movies are only part of the Bob Hope story; he has starred on radio and television, as well as on the stage, but there are few comedians who have made as many hot comedies over as long a period as Hope.

Probably the best-remembered of these comedies are the Road films, which Hope made with Bing Crosby and Dorothy Lamour. The first of the lot was *Road to Singapore,* made in 1940, in which Hope and Crosby encounter Lamour as a sarong-clad beauty on an island in the Pacific. The formula of Hope wisecracking, Crosby as a relaxed straight man who broke into song now and then, and Lamour as background proved successful, and the film was followed by *Road to Zanzibar, Road to Morocco, Road to Utopia,* and others. As time went on, the plots got more informal and the atmosphere rather casual. Camels would talk, Hope would turn to the camera when Crosby began to sing and suggest that the audience go out for popcorn, and there were plenty of in jokes about the Crosby and Hope business interests. The last in the series was *Road to Hong Kong* in 1962.

Hope made many other comedies, with a large number of leading ladies. Neither the plots nor the characters of the Hope films are worth much time; what carries the films is the amazing Bob Hope talent for rattling off a string of wisecracks. You might not remember much of a Bob Hope movie an hour or two after you got home, but he kept you laughing while you were in the theater, and that was good enough. The fact that Bob Hope is as big a hit in the 1970s as he was in the 1930s speaks for itself.

A comedian who has lasted nearly as long as Hope is Red Skelton, whose career in the movies (and later in television) stretched from the 1940s to the 1960s. Skelton was one of the most durable performers in the MGM stable during the years when that studio was one of the Hollywood giants. His peak period as a film comedian was the 1940s and 1950s, when he was the star of such movies as *Whistling in Dixie, Whistling in Brooklyn, Whistling in the Dark, The Fuller Brush Man, The Yellow Cab Man* and many more. After the movie glow faded, Skelton had a highly successful television career, doing a weekly show for twenty years before his network called it quits.

Despite Skelton's undoubted success, there was always a feeling that he could have accomplished even more with his talents. A hint of what might have been came at the very end of his performing days, when Skelton appeared in a two-man pantomime show with the world-famous French mime, Marcel Marceau. Skelton was not quite up to Marceau's level—few performers are—but he made a respectable showing. Many of his fans were left wondering what Skelton might have done if he had not been just a part of the well-oiled MGM money-making machine, but had had the same opportunity as Chaplin and Keaton did in the early days to find his own way. (The television show, in which Skelton did have that opportunity, was no fair comparison because the accent in television is on quantity, not quality.)

The same harsh judgment—good, but could have been better—is made by most critics about the career of another American funny man, Danny Kaye. He had every talent in the world, including the ability to sing nonsense songs at a faster-than-light pace, a rubber face, and an excellent sense of timing, Kaye certainly cannot be called a failure; he has delighted audiences all over the world for decades. Yet considering what he might have accomplished, the comedy films made by Kaye fall short, and usually for the same reason—they get mushy and sentimental when they should be sharp and pointed.

The best of the Kaye films are those in which he makes fun of the high and the mighty. *The Inspector General,* made in 1949 and probably Kaye's best comedy, has him playing a schnook in nineteenth-century Russia who gets mistaken for the inspector general who is feared by all corrupt officials. Since all the officials in the town of Brodny, where this mistake occurs, are corrupt, the schnook suddenly finds himself getting treatment fit for a king. Despite a few weak moments, *The Inspector General* is pretty much a roaring success, with Kaye getting excellent assistance from such talented performers as Walter Slezak and Elsa Lanchester.

Also high on the list of Kaye successes is *The Court Jester,* in which Kaye plays a poor bumpkin in medieval England who is mistaken for a court jester whose sideline is assassinating kings. The plot has something to do with restoring an infant king to his rightful throne and the finale is an all-out fight in the castle with Kaye assisted by midgets (it sounds funnier than it looks on film), but the real fun comes in such scenes as Kaye being given the bum's rush through a supposedly digni-

Danny Kaye.
Dressed up as *The Court Jester,* he is offering an obviously lame excuse to Cecil Parker, while Basil Rathbone, the villain, listens at right. (*Paramount, 1956*)

fied ceremony of knighthood and Kaye jousting with a suit of armor that has become magnetized. But the film has the same flaws that loom larger in other Kaye comedies—too much plot, too many second-rate songs, too many pretty costumes, and not enough sharp wit. It is fair to wonder how much more Danny Kaye might have accomplished if he had come along at a different period in movie history.

12

Modern Times

It is now generally agreed that the great days of movie comedy are over forever, because the traditional training grounds for comedians no longer exist. The movies never really trained their own comedians. The great comics have come from the British music halls or American vaudeville, from Broadway or from night clubs. The movies killed vaudeville, television has crippled the night-club business, Broadway is in decline, and even the movies have had to cut way back because of television. And television does not create talent, but consumes it.

A very few comedians, such as Red Skelton, Lucille Ball, and Carol Burnett, have the ability to last on television for many seasons. But most television comedians come and go in just a few years, their material used up and their bodies exhausted by the strain of meeting the weekly deadline. And without exception, attempts by the movies to cash in on the success of television comedians have been complete failures, resulting in such completely forgettable movies as George Gobel's *I Married a Woman* and Rowan and Martin's *The Maltese Bippy*. Even Lucille Ball, who first honed her comedy talents in the movies before becoming a smash hit on television, has not made any memorable movie in her occasional return to films.

But despite all the obstacles, including greatly reduced movie schedules and inflated costs, there are still a few talented performers carrying on the tradition of great movie comedy.

Jerry Lewis is one of them, and perhaps the most controversial of the lot. There are some critics, particularly in France, who believe that Jerry Lewis is one of the finest comic minds of the movies. There are plenty of people who will come out to see a Jerry Lewis movie—one of his boasts is that none of his films has ever lost money. The majority view is that Jerry Lewis is an underachiever—a funny man who could have been much funnier than he is, and whose films are marred by too much mugging and cheap, meaningless gags.

Jerry Lewis was originally half of the comedy team of Martin and Lewis. Dean Martin was the straight man, feeding Jerry lines and singing an occasional song. The team began in small night clubs just after World War II and very quickly shot to the top of the night-club circuit. They were brought to Hollywood in 1949 by producer Hal Wallis, who started them in a film called *My Friend Irma*, which was based on a popular radio show of the time. They stole the movie and their film career was off to a running start.

After a series of comedies, generally on make-fun-of-the-military themes (*At War with the Army, Sailor Beware*), Martin and Lewis established themselves as one of the biggest box-office attractions in Hollywood (although the fans liked the films better than the critics did). But signs of a clash of personalities appeared, and the team split in the late 1950s. Dean Martin went on to a highly successful career in both movies and television. Jerry Lewis also became a star on his own, directing and

Jerry Lewis.
In *Living It Up,* as a small-town boy who gets to the big town by pretending to have a rare disease. The girl is Kathryn Grant. (*Paramount, 1954*)

acting in a series of film comedies, which he turned out at the rate of one a year.

Reaction to all these films can be summarized briefly: the fans came and laughed, the critics acknowledged some good points, but generally held their noses.

Only time will tell who is right—remember, Laurel and Hardy did not win critical acclaim until their career was almost over—but at this point it seems that the thumbs-down verdict is correct. Jerry Lewis is funny, all right; there are hilarious moments in every one of his films. But Jerry Lewis has not produced the great comedies that one might have expected of him.

In particular, he has not created the great comedy character that one could have expected—a character that could have rivaled Lloyd or Langdon. True, the character that Jerry Lewis plays in every movie is the same—a hopeless fool with a nasal accent who is despised by everyone around him and whose name is usually Irving. The setting can be a hotel (*The Bellboy*), a hospital (*The Disorderly Orderly*), a department store (*Who's Minding the Store?*) or a college (*The Nutty Professor*), but the plot is always the same: the poor fool wins his way to fame and fortune (and the pretty girl) in spite of everything. That might not sound like much, but it is the same basic plot that Harold Lloyd or Buster Keaton used to create film classics. Jerry Lewis's films fall short of that.

Jerry Lewis has two faults. First, he does not respect his film character in the way that Chaplin, Keaton, or Lloyd did. When they created a character, they made sure that the character did nothing to destroy the image on the screen. Jerry Lewis will give up that kind of consistency to get a quick laugh; his fool is a fool one minute and a wise man the next minute. Sure, Lewis gets the laughs he is after, but truly great comedy is more than gags that get laughs.

The other fault is serious only because of the era in which Jerry Lewis has made his films. Lewis does not seem to be able to make a comedy that works for the length of a feature film. Many critics have remarked that his comedies get off to a great start and then begin to fall down after about twenty minutes. Well, twenty minutes is about the length of a two-reel comedy of the sort that made the reputation of Chaplin, Keaton, Lloyd, Laurel and Hardy, and most of the other screen comedy greats. And it has been noted that many of these greats had trouble adjusting to the full-length format; many critics have said that Chaplin and Laurel and Hardy never made the adjustment.

But unlike Chaplin and the others, Jerry Lewis never had a chance to make two-reelers, a kind of film that had faded out by the time he came to the screen. Perhaps if he had been able to make shorter films, he would have done well enough so that critics would overlook the faults of his full-length films. As it is, we will never know. We can only be grateful for the very many funny moments that Jerry Lewis has put on the screen, and knowing enough to tell the difference between Lewis at his best and Lewis at his not-so-good. Like the little girl in the nursery rhyme, when he is good, he is very, very good, and when he is bad he is horrid. Jerry Lewis must be accepted for what he is—a flawed genius.

At this time, the man who reigns as the top film comedian in America is another actor who plays poor fools: Woody Allen. But where Jerry Lewis is generally viewed as a failure (although a financially successful failure), Woody Allen is viewed as one of the greatest successes in films today. Certainly, few comedians aside from Chaplin can match Allen for versatility. Woody Allen writes his own scripts, directs his own movies, plays the leading role, and even, in some films, provides the musical background. (He plays good jazz saxophone.) Starting as just another nightclub comic, Woody Allen has climbed to the top of the comedy heap.

If there is one feature that sets Woody Allen apart from other film comedians, it is the intellectual nature of his comedy.

120

Woody Allen is always parodying film comedies (and tragedies) of the past. Usually the parody comes in bits and pieces, but one Allen film, *Play It Again, Sam,* was built entirely around Humphrey Bogart and the hero he played in the film classic, *Casablanca.* Like W. C. Fields and the Marx Brothers, Allen is not too concerned about keeping the plots of his films in apple-pie shape; most of the time, the plots are just excuses for stringing together gags.

In *Bananas,* the plot has something to do with a revolution in a Latin American country. In *Sleeper,* the plot is about Woody awakening to find that he has slept two hundred years into the future. It doesn't really matter. The whole point is that Woody Allen will get into the expected set of absurd situations (posing as a robot in *Sleeper,* living in the mountains with a rebel band in *Bananas*) that allow plenty of sight gags and funny lines. To watch a Woody Allen movie is to see what amounts to a brief history of film comedy. Everything from the Mack Sennett style of slapstick to the most sophisticated kind of screwball comedy humor is wrapped into one package. The more you know about films, the more you will appreciate a Woody Allen film, but he can be funny even for audiences who don't have too much knowledge of past comedy greats. Woody Allen's film career, excellent as it has been so far, is just beginning (his first film under his own direction was not made until 1969), and there is a distinct feeling that the best is yet to come.

Another director-actor who is considered to be at the top of today's film comedy field is a Frenchman whose name may be unfamiliar to many Americans: Jacques Tati. While Tati's films are often shown at film festivals and in big-city revival theaters, he has not really become well known in most of the United States. Yet those who have seen his films believe that they deserve to be ranked among the best film comedies of all time.

Tati tells his stories through the character of Mr. Hulot, a Frenchman in clothes that are a shade too small, with a pipe

Sleeper.
Woody Allen, disguised as a robot in the twenty-second century, is in danger of having his head removed for repair. (*United Artists, 1973*)

Jacques Tati.
Mr. Hulot, the quizzical man in the middle with the pipe, is in another fix in *My Uncle*. (*Continental Distributing, 1958*)

poking off at an odd angle, who has a most peculiar walk—on tiptoe and with a bounce, as if his feet were mounted on springs. The constant theme of the Tati films is the unsuccessful encounter of Mr. Hulot with the modern, efficient world. In *Mr. Hulot's Holiday,* the Tati character is out of place among a crowd of people who are working hard at making their brief two-week vacations a success. In *My Uncle,* Mr. Hulot has disastrous encounters with a modern automated home and a modern automated plastics factory. In *Traffic,* Mr. Hulot tries to deliver a modern camper to an auto show; the effort takes the entire film, and the camper never gets there. In *Playtime,* a group of tourists hurtle through an ultramodern Paris that has lost the charm which made tourists want to come to Paris in the first place.

Most critics praise Tati for the brilliance of his themes and his gags, but it must be said that Tati films are not easy for the casual viewer. Even though the films are French, language is not the problem, because Tati tells his stories almost without words—an amazing feat in these days, when sound is taken for granted. What makes Tati difficult is his quick, subtle style. A Tati gag is on the screen and then off again so quickly that the audience hardly has time to laugh. For that reason, Tati demands a lot of attention; you have to be alert and on your toes to appreciate what he is doing.

Tati is often compared to Chaplin, because both comedians have the same basic theme, the little man in conflict with society. In Tati's case, it is a computerized society, where everything is hustle and bustle, and there is no room for the kind of amiable stroller like Mr. Hulot. In just the same way, Chaplin's Tramp was always out of place in the polite society of his time.

But that kind of comparison doesn't really mean much in talking about comedy films. The only real test is whether a comedian can make his audiences laugh. Chaplin passed that test with flying colors, which is the only reason why critics today write deep theoretical articles about the inner meaning of his comedies. Tati passes the test, too, although he is not as easy to appreciate at first viewing as Chaplin. You might have to see a Tati film two or three times to really roar at the gags, but there are a lot worse ways to spend your time than seeing a Tati film two or three times. Jacques Tati carries on the great tradition of film comedy.

So does Woody Allen, although he makes the same kind of hard demands on his audiences. While Tati demands frequent viewings, Woody Allen requires a lot of information about movies of the past and problems of today. It is a nervous, busy kind of humor, fitted to our nervous, busy time. Woody Allen makes fun of Jewish mothers, computers, McDonald's hamburgers, Albert Shanker, *Playboy* magazine, and other institutions of our time. Tati plays an innocent character, but Woody Allen plays a sophisticated character. Both manage to be quite funny.

So maybe it is too early to say that the great days of film comedy are completely finished. One way or another, funny men keep coming along, and audiences find films that keep them laughing. Of late, the movies have made several fairly successful efforts to revive the spirit of the past, in such films as *The Great Race* and *Those Magnificent Men in Their Flying Machines* that try to repeat the same madcap slapstick of the Mack Sennett days. The effort never quite succeeds because the films are too conscious that they are imitations; there is never the carefree attitude that made the Sennett films so hilarious.

But, looking back, it seems to our eyes that the era when the Sennett films were made was a daredevil, carefree time, very much different from our troubled and complex era. If we find less to laugh at on the screen, it might be that we take our world too seriously. More than ever, we need great comedians to provide the laughter that makes life worth while. And we can look to the movies, past and present, to provide those vital laughs.

Index

Edward Edelson

Although Edward Edelson spends most of his working hours as the science editor of the New York *Daily News,* he still manages to find time to watch plenty of old movies. A graduate of New York University and a Sloan-Rockefeller Fellow in the Advanced Science Writing Program at Columbia University, Mr. Edelson now lives in Jamaica, New York, with his wife and three children. His previous books include *Great Monsters from the Movies, The Book of Prophecy,* and *Visions of Tomorrow.*

Cumberland Trail Library System
Flora, Illinois 62839